USING THE NEW AACR2

An expert systems approach to choice of points

USING THE NEW AACR2

AACR2

An expert systems approach to choice of access points

David Smith
*Principal Lecturer, Information and Library Studies Group,
Leeds Metropolitan University*

David Evans
*formerly Senior Lecturer, Information and Library Studies Group,
Leeds Metropolitan University*

Alan Poulter
*Lecturer, Department of Information and Library Studies,
Loughborough University of Technology*

Malcolm Shaw
*Principal Lecturer and Curriculum Development Manager,
Leeds Metropolitan University*

LIBRARY ASSOCIATION PUBLISHING
LONDON

© Library Association Publishing Ltd 1980, 1993

Published by
Library Association Publishing Ltd
7 Ridgmount Street
London WC1E 7AE

First published 1980 as *Using AACR2: a step-by-step algorithmic approach*
This revised edition 1993

British Library Cataloguing in Publication Data

Smith, David
    Using the New AACR 2: Expert Systems
    Approach to Choice of Access Points. —
    2Rev.ed
    I. Title
    025.32

    ISBN 1-85604-086-0

Typeset in Times by Library Association Publishing Ltd
Printed and made in Great Britain by Bookcraft (Bath) Ltd

CONTENTS

PREFACE TO THIS EDITION

The algorithmic approach to the use of AACR2 has proved very successful in the classroom, when used with both undergraduate and postgraduate students. When the first edition was published we received several appreciative letters from working cataloguers and training officers, who had also found it a useful tool.

The Library Association requested a new edition of the algorithms when the 1988 revision of the code was published. Various crises at my university meant that this edition was at regular intervals put on the back boiler. I am grateful to my co-authors, and to Barbara Jover of LA Publishing, for their patience and support. I think my colleagues will agree with me, in some ways doing a revision of the algorithms was more difficult than doing the original!

By including an expert system as well as a hard-copy algorithm (which I understand is a first for LA Publishing), we have come up to date with modern developments in cataloguing in at least one major respect.[1] However, perhaps not in others. The text was almost ready for delivery to the Library Association when I received, courtesy of the LA and the Joint Steering Committee, a batch of revisions to the code. This called for some fast decision making as well as close study.

On the grounds that I can see no major changes in these revisions, and that as far as I am aware few, if any, catalogue tutors update their teaching sets with the revisions, I have decided to keep this edition based on the 1988 revision itself. The algorithm is not meant to be a substitute for the code; AACR2 should be checked when a final decision on a particular algorithm is reached, and I hope changes can and will be picked up in that way.

I am grateful to Anne Lunn for working through our new algorithms to check that they worked. The algorithms have been checked, double-checked, and triple-checked; but if any mistakes have crept through, the responsibility is mine.

Dave Smith
Leeds Metropolitan University

[1] Note: the printed version of *Using the new AACR2* can be used independently of the disk

PREFACE TO THE FIRST EDITION

This work had its origins in a discussion between David Smith, a lecturer in the School of Librarianship of Leeds Polytechnic, and Malcolm Shaw of the Polytechnic's Educational Technology Unit. The theme of the discussion was the need to evolve a teaching method for introducing students to what were (for the uninitiated at least) the bewildering ramifications of rules in the first edition of the Anglo-American Cataloguing Rules. Malcolm Shaw suggested the possibility of an algorithmic approach, i.e. a decision-making flowchart which would enable the Rules to be applied in a sequence of logical steps.

An algorithm to Chapter 1 of the Rules was drafted, and used for a time in the School of Librarianship. Further development was deferred, however, because of the imminence of a second edition of AACR. Subsequently David Evans and Bill Dent, also of the Leeds School of Librarianship, became interested in the project and the present collaboration resulted, once the text of the second edition became available. The general division of work was that Malcolm Shaw drafted the outline of the algorithms for all the chapters covered by this introductory text – Chapters 21–5. David Smith collaborated with him in producing the detailed version for Chapter 21, and Bill Dent fulfilled a similar role in the cases of Chapters 22–5. David Evans collected the accompanying examples and prepared the commentaries which relate to them. Bill Dent wrote the various introductory sections. However, at every stage there were discussions and mutually agreed amendments to the contents. The results amply fulfil AACR's definition of 'shared responsibility': unquestionably a situation in which Rule 21.6C2 may be deemed to apply!

The work is intended primarily for students of librarianship who are in process of initiation into the techniques of cataloguing. However, it is hoped that it will also be of value to practising cataloguers who are 'converting' from the use of AACR1, or some other code of practice, to AACR2. It is specifically a guide to the application of Chapters 21–5 of the second edition of the Anglo-American Cataloguing Rules, but there is an underlying intention to show that 'author cataloguing' involves a sequence of logical steps in arriving at the appropriate entries and headings for a document. At the same time it must be stressed that the work does relate directly to AACR2 as it stands. It has not been the intention to produce a general manual of cataloguing practice, nor was it considered appropriate to attempt to 'improve' upon the Rules.

AACR2EXPERT

Using the AACR2EXPERT floppy disk

AACR2EXPERT should work on any PC compatible, with at least 512K RAM and running under DOS 3.2 or above.

Start up your computer and when you see the DOS prompt put the AACR2EXPERT disk into the A disk drive. If the prompt is not A> then type A: and press Return. To activate AACR2EXPERT type AACR2 and press Return. After the title screen you will be offered a choice of four different cataloguing topics, access points, uniform titles, corporate and personal names, on which to receive advice.

Choose a cataloguing topic by typing in its number and pressing Return. You will see two 'reading' messages, for questions and rules (these are explained in the Introduction to AACR2EXPERT section, below). You will be presented with a question. Answer it either Yes or No and press Return. Abbreviations Y and N are not acceptable. Answer subsequent questions in the same way.

At certain times AACR2EXPERT will conclude that an applicable rule from AACR2 should be consulted, and give a summary of that rule's recommendations. Other conclusions that AACR2EXPERT reaches will also be presented. Press any key to move on, after viewing AACR2EXPERT's conclusions.

The consultation will end when AACR2EXPERT presents you with the last applicable rule from AACR2 relevant to your cataloguing query. A list of the facts AACR2EXPERT has found will then be presented. Press any key to view more of these. You will be returned to the screen offering advice on cataloguing topics.

To find out why AACR2EXPERT has asked a question, type WHY and press Return.

To find out what facts AACR2EXPERT has discovered, type FACTS and press Return, when being asked a question.

To quit any cataloguing topic in AACR2EXPERT, type QUIT and press Return, when being asked a question.

You are advised to make a backup copy of the disk.

If you have a hard disk, copy the files from the disk to a directory on the hard disk. AACR2EXPERT can then be run from this directory.

Please report problems to:

Alan Poulter
c/o Library Association Publishing
7 Ridgmount Street
London WC1E 7AE

Introduction to AACR2EXPERT

AACR2EXPERT is a type of computer program known as an expert system. An expert system attempts to emulate the expertise of a human expert. Most expert systems come in two parts, a knowledge base, which contains human expert knowledge in a structure which is usable by a computer, and a shell, which uses the knowledge base to form expert judgements.

On the floppy diskette are five files, one for the expert system shell, AACR2.EXE, and four others:

ACCESS.KB	–	knowledge about access points
TITLE.KB	–	knowledge about uniform titles
BODY.KB	–	knowledge about headings for corporate bodies
NAME.KB	–	knowledge about headings for personal names

These four files (all with KB extensions) make up the knowledge base. ACCESS.KB is for Algorithm 1 on access points. The other three files, TITLE.KB, BODY.KB and NAME.KB, are for entries under uniform title, corporate bodies or personal names, the three parts of Algorithm 2.

The shell was written using version 5.5 of Borland Turbo Pascal. It was developed on an Amstrad 1640 running under DOS 5.0.

The knowledge base files can be examined with any word processor or text editor. Follow the normal procedure for loading in a text file, giving one of the .KB files as the text file to be loaded. Take care not to make changes to the original copy of any .KB file, however.

Each knowledge base file consists of a number of questions and production rules (as distinct from cataloguing rules). Each production rule is numbered, and ends with a '*'. Each production rule has the same format:

IF condition 1
{AND condition 2}
. . .
{AND condition x}
THEN conclusion 1
{AND conclusion 2}
. . .
{AND conclusion x}

The curly brackets { and } indicate optional elements. Thus each production rule must contain at least one condition and at least one conclusion. If the condition(s) of a production rule become true, then the conclusion(s) of a production rule become true.

Each condition and conclusion consists of a variable name, the word 'IS' and a value. Thus an example of a production rule with two conditions and three conclusions would be:

3
if title change is yes
and serial is yes
then changed title rule is Rule 21.2C1
and separate main entry is for each title
and change in title is checked
*

The conditions are 'title change is yes' and 'serial is yes'. The conclusions are 'changed title rule is Rule 21.2C1', 'separate main entry is for each title' and 'change in title is checked'. A production rule links a particular set of conditions which need to be true to prove a particular set of conclusions.

During a particular session, if a variable has a value it is known as a fact. Thus, for the example production rule above, if the two conditions were known facts, then the three variables in the conclusions would also be facts. A production rule then is a statement in English-like form of the logical connections of facts.

Values for variables come either from those variables occurring in the conclusion to a production rule or from information obtained from the user of the expert system. If the value of a variable can be obtained from a user then a question exists for it. Questions have a fixed format:

QUESTION variable
[text of question]
*

Thus an example of a question would be:
question serial

Is the work a serial?
*

Answers to a question are limited to the different values the rules give for that question. All questions in AACR2EXPERT expect either yes or no answers.

This shell works by choosing a goal for the user's consultation. The shell then checks through the production rules for the first one in which the chosen goal is a conclusion. It then attempts to prove or disprove the conditions of the production rule. This may mean asking questions of the user or it may mean proving another production rule which has as one of its conclusions a condition in the first production rule. This process is known as backward chaining, i.e. working backwards from a known goal.

This process of checking production rules which have the goal in a conclusion continues until a production rule is found for which all the conditions are true. This production rule then provides the final value for the sought goal. In AACR2EXPERT, the goal is always to find a value for 'last applicable Rule'.

The algorithms in the flowcharts have been translated into production rules. Each path through each of the flowcharts should exist in the form of production rules. One of the uses of AACR2EXPERT is then to form an alternative method of consulting the algorithms, which does not demand skipping about between the pages in the book.

Early research into the applications of expert systems in cataloguing involved using parts of these algorithms as a source for knowledge bases. An excellent overview of this research is provided by Davies, 1992. AACR2EXPERT is the first generally available expert system for cataloguing, using all the algorithms in the book.

Another usage would be to investigate the working of expert systems. The simplest knowledge base is that for personal name headings (NAME.KB) and the workings of this knowledge base should be the easiest to follow. It is possible to load any of the knowledge bases into a commercial expert system shell, rather than use the basic shell provided. You would need to consult the documentation of that commercial shell, in order to know how its rule files needed to be structured. You would then need to modify the .KB files accordingly with a word processor or a text editor, so that the commercial shell could read them.

Reference

Davies, R., *Expert systems and cataloguing*. In Morris, Anne (ed.), *The application of expert systems in libraries and information centres*, London, Bowker-Saur, 1992, 133–66.

AUTHOR CATALOGUES AND AUTHOR CATALOGUING

A library catalogue consists of a file of *entries* or *records* of materials contained in a library. Each entry contains a certain amount of information about the item recorded – sufficient to:

(a) Identify the document. i.e. To distinguish it from any other item and, further, to distinguish one edition or version of a work from other editions or versions of the same work, and

(b) Characterize the document. i.e. Convey some impression of the nature of the work – both its physical make-up and its intellectual content.

Note that the term 'document' is used to imply an item of library material in any form: a book, a piece of music, a map, a sound recording, etc, etc.

The information which is contained in a catalogue entry is called the *description*. It comprises all the information contained in the entry other than the *heading*: the data element by which the entry is arranged in the catalogue file. The process of preparing the description is referred to, naturally enough, as *descriptive cataloguing*. A typical catalogue entry might appear thus:

The description

{

```
?? Heading ??

    Four hundred years of English education
[text] / by W.H.G. Armytage. – 2nd ed. –
Cambridge : Cambridge U.P., 1970.
    xii, 353 p. ; 22 cm.
    First published 1964.
    ISBN 0-521-09583-2
```

The amount of descriptive detail which is necessary in a catalogue entry will vary according to the size and purpose of the library. Further, the order and fashion in which the description is presented is not, in itself, of any great significance. However, it may be apparent that it is desirable for such data to be given in a standard and consistent manner, not merely within one particular catalogue but in all catalogues and similar bibliographic listings. Consequently there are codes of rules which prescribe the way in which cataloguers should express the descriptive data. In the second edition of the Anglo-American Cataloguing Rules (subsequently referred to as AACR2), with which this text is concerned, Part I sets out the rules for the descriptive cataloguing of all types of library materials. However, the present work is concerned with the *choice* and *form* of headings in 'author' and 'title' catalogues.

The headings which are assigned to the catalogue entries described above will depend upon the objectives of the catalogues involved. Broadly, the basic objectives of library catalogues are:

(a) To enable the location of library materials on a particular subject or subject area. e.g. Materials on underground railways, electric railways, railway locomotives, or on railways in general, or, for that matter, on the subject of transportation in general. The kind of catalogue which provides for this sort of approach is, obviously enough, a *subject catalogue*, in which the headings will be labels which identify, in one way or another, the subject matter of the document recorded. The subject catalogue and its construction is outside the scope of the present text.

(b) To permit the location of a particular document, about which some precise identifying feature is known. e.g. The name of the person or persons, organization or organizations, in some way responsible for the creation of the document; its title; or the title of the series of documents to which it belongs. An alternative way of describing this objective would be to say that the library catalogue should provide for a *known-item search*. The kind of catalogue which caters for this sort of approach is generally referred to as an 'author' or 'author/title' catalogue. The headings in such a catalogue will, then, be names of people or organizations responsible for the content of documents and the titles of both individual items and series of items. It is with the establishment of such headings that the present text is concerned: more particularly, with Part II of AACR2, which governs the choice of these headings and the form which they take.

Before proceeding further it will be useful to define more precisely the terms 'author' and 'author catalogue'.

Authorship
'Personal author' is defined by Rule 21.1A1 of AACR2 in the following way:

A personal author is the person chiefly responsible for the creation of the intellectual content of a work. For example, writers of books and composers of music are the authors of the works they create; compilers of bibliographies are the authors of those bibliographies; cartographers are the authors of their maps; artists and photographers of the works they create. In addition, in certain cases, performers are the authors of sound recordings, films, and videorecordings.

Further, in Rule 21.1B2, AACR2 recognizes that in certain instances corporate bodies (or organizations) may be regarded as being, effectively, 'authors' of certain categories of document which emanate from them. Thus 'author', in the sense in which it is used in the Rules and in this text, has a much wider connotation than merely 'writer of the text of a book'.

'Author catalogue'
It follows, from what has been said above, that a so-called 'author catalogue' is rather more than its name suggests. It will contain entries under the names of people (and organizations) who are in some way responsible for the existence of a document, and via whom a catalogue user may reasonably consult the catalogue in making a 'known-item' search.

In addition, as indicated earlier, the 'author catalogue' may well include entries under the titles of works and under the titles of series to which those works belong. These 'title' entries may be arranged in a separate sequence to form an independent 'title catalogue', but are more often filed in the same sequence as the 'author' entries to produce a single alphabetical sequence of 'author' and 'title' entries. This is usually referred to as simply an 'author catalogue', but it would be more exactly described as an 'author/title catalogue'.

It should be remembered that most 'author catalogues' are multiple entry catalogues. That is to say, they will usually contain a number of entries for the same item under different headings.

e.g. A book written by two authors, with significant illustrative content by a third person, and belonging to a bibliographic series such as 'The new naturalist series', might well have five entries in the 'author catalogue': under the names of its two authors, under the name of the illustrator, under its title, and under the title of the series. Generally one of these entries will be regarded as the *main entry* for the document: the principal entry; that which will contain the fullest information in a catalogue which (perhaps to economize in the use of space) does not give full descriptive details in all entries. The cataloguer will attempt to ensure that the heading of the main entry is the principal identifying feature for the work. The additional entries made for an item (i.e. those other than the main entry) are referred to as *added entries*. They may contain rather less descriptive information than the main entry for the document.

The convention of having an 'author catalogue' made up of main and added entries is long established. It probably dates from the nineteenth century when catalogues were frequently in book format, produced by conventional printing methods, and it was desirable to restrict the physical size of catalogues as much as possible. Whatever the origin of the convention, the need to distinguish a main entry from the other entries made for a work is questioned with increasing frequency. Certainly the selection of the main entry heading from a number of headings which may be considered to be necessary for a work is often the most difficult part of the author cataloguing process. Paragraph 0.5 of the general introduction to AACR2 makes a brief mention of the principle of main entry, and fuller discussions may be found in the other readings cited at the end of this introductory section. It is not felt that this is an appropriate place to debate the question. However, it should be noted that whilst distinguishing between main and added entries may make little difference to the effectiveness of an individual library catalogue, the assignment of a main entry *heading* is an attempt to establish a standard identifying label by which a work will be listed in *all* bibliographic listings – library catalogues, bibliographies, publishers' lists, etc. – not all of which are multiple entry listings.

In addition to main and added entries an 'author catalogue' will contain *references*. These may be *see* or *see also* references. The purposes of the two kinds of references are quite distinct. A *see* reference is a firm direction away from a heading which is not used and will never be used to a preferred heading. e.g.

> Clemens, Samuel Langhorne
> *see*
> Twain, Mark.

This implies that the author's real name – Samuel Langhorne Clemens – will never be used as a heading for entries: his pseudonym – Mark Twain – will always be used in its stead.

A *see also* reference is employed to link two headings which are (or may be) both used as headings for entries, and between which some connection exists. e.g.

> Great Britain. *Countryside Commission*
> *see also*
> Great Britain. *National Parks Commission*
> for publications before 1967.

It should be stressed that references are used only for the two purposes outlined above. They are not used to provide access points to a document from alternative identifying features. e.g. A work entitled 'The Penguin book of Elizabethan verse', compiled by Edward Lucie-Smith, would (according to AACR2) have its main entry under its title. An added entry would certainly be made under the heading for the compiler – Lucie-Smith, Edward. A *see* reference would be made to direct the catalogue user away from the unused form of Lucie-Smith's name to the preferred form i.e.

Smith, Edward Lucie-
see
Lucie-Smith, Edward.

A reference should *not* be used, however, to provide access via Lucie-Smith's name. i.e.

Lucie-Smith, Edward
see
The Penguin book of Elizabethan verse.

This would imply that the heading – Lucie-Smith, Edward – will never be used as a heading in its own right and that the name will only ever be associated in the catalogue with this one publication. This is clearly absurd since the individual concerned may have in the past, or may in the future, be responsible for other works recorded in the catalogue.

The need for a code of cataloguing rules
An 'author catalogue' is, then, a record of the materials held in a library, with entries under a variety of 'author' and title headings via which a catalogue user may reasonably search for a work.

Whilst an 'author catalogue' is clearly an important element in the effective functioning of a library, its construction would seem to be a fairly straightforward process of listing or inventorying. Therefore the need for an extensive code of practice such as the Anglo-American Cataloguing Rules may come as something of a surprise to the newcomer to cataloguing. It would seem possible to base the construction of such a catalogue upon a single, simple, direction to the effect of:

Enter a work under the name of its author (the person responsible for its creation): in the absence of any attribution of authorship, enter the work under its title.

For a not insignificant proportion of the material which most libraries catalogue this simple direction may, indeed, suffice. However, it is equally probable that in compiling even a very short list of 10 or 20 books and/or other library materials there will arise situations in which we must take decisions beyond the terms of this simple direction. Naturally, the need for these extra decisions increases when our listing consists of thousands, or tens of thousands, of items – as in a large library catalogue.

The instances in which these further decisions must be taken may be analysed as follows:

(a) When the cataloguer is *uncertain whom to regard as 'author'*, e.g. when a number of people share the responsibility for the contents of a work. Instances of this are when two or more individuals jointly prepare a work; or where a work is a collection of contributions from a number of different people. Another example of where this problem arises is in the case of what AACR2 refers to as 'mixed authorship'. That is to say, where two or more people have contributed to the contents of a work in different ways. Instances of this would be a work in which one person contributed the words and another composed the music; or in which one person provided the illustrations and another the accompanying text.

It is worth noting that the question really at issue here is that concerning the main entry heading. If one assumes a multiple entry catalogue, one presumes that entries will be made under any of the names or other identifying features via which a document may be sought. Therefore, in asking 'Whom do I regard as author?' one is really asking 'Whom (or what) do I select as main entry heading, and, under whom (or what) shall I make added entries?'.

(b) When there is *uncertainty concerning the name to be used as the heading for an author*. Specifically, these uncertainties may arise because:

    (i) An author has used different names, e.g. family name *and* title of nobility – Anthony Eden *and* Lord Avon; real name *and* pseudonym – Charles Dodgson *and* Lewis Carroll; maiden *and* married name(s) – Jacqueline Bouvier, Jacqueline Kennedy, Jacqueline Onassis; and so on.

    (ii) Different forms of the same name may occur, e.g. variations in fullness – A. Conan Doyle *and* Sir Arthur Conan Doyle; the name in different languages – Jeanne d'Arc *and* Joan of Arc; different transliterations of the same name – Mohammed, Mahommed, Mahomet; and so on.

    (iii) The entry element for the name is not obvious, e.g. compound names – Cecil Woodham-Smith: entered as Woodham-Smith, Cecil, or as Smith, Cecil Woodham-?; names with prefixes – Charles de Gaulle: entered as de Gaulle, Charles, or as Gaulle, Charles de?; a given name or by-name – William of Malmesbury: entered under Malmesbury, William of, or in direct order?

    Generally names from different cultures may pose problems to the cataloguer. e.g. a Chinese name such as Foo Kwac Wah: which part of the name is to be regarded as 'surname' and the entry element for the name?

    It should be borne in mind that uncertainties about names apply equally – or perhaps to an even greater extent – to corporate names: names of organizations and other bodies. e.g. the British Department of Education and Science: should it be entered as – Department of Education and Science, or as Education and Science, Department of, or under some other form of name?

    Similarly, the Association of Assistant Librarians is a sub-section of the (British) Library Association. Should this organization be entered directly under its own name or as a sub-heading of the parent organization – Library Association. *Association of Assistant Librarians*?

(c) Finally, when an entry is required under the title (either as a main or added entry heading) the cataloguer may need to establish *which title* to use, in that the titles of works may alter in the same way as the names of authors. Consider the hundreds of different titles which have appeared on different versions and editions of the Bible and its constituent parts over the centuries, or the many different titles which have been applied to editions of anonymous classics such as *The Arabian nights*.

The problems outlined and illustrated above are, in themselves, very minor matters. However, it is perhaps apparent that in a library catalogue containing many thousands of entries, built over a long period of time, by many different hands, unless these problems – small though they may be – are solved in a consistent fashion then the catalogue as a whole will be inconsistent and contradictory and unpredictable and, as a consequence, inefficient and unreliable.

The purpose of a code of rules for 'author' cataloguing is, then, to establish a consistent and standard practice in the *choice* of headings and in establishing the *form* which those headings will take. The primary objective is the obvious one of achieving consistency and uniformity within a particular catalogue. However, there is an underlying objective of much broader significance: the establishment of a standard practice in library catalogues and other bibliographic listings on a national and, hopefully, an international scale. In short, to ensure that a document will be entered in precisely the same fashion in any catalogue or listing in which it appears. Clearly it would be convenient for a number of reasons if this were so. For example it would simplify the checking of bibliographic data and it would facilitate the interchange of cataloguing data between libraries and cataloguing agencies.

Evolution of AACR2

It would seem that libraries have employed cataloguing rules – albeit perhaps very simple 'house rules' of purely local significance – for hundreds of years. Presumably from the time that the size of collections necessitated some measure of sophistication in the way in which they were recorded.

However, it was not until the second half of the nineteenth century that codes of rules with greater than local influence began to emerge. The starting point, what may be regarded as the foundation of modern 'author cataloguing' practice, was the publication in 1841 of 'Rules for the compilation of the printed catalogues of the British Museum'. Subsequently various other collections of rules of national or international significance appeared. C. A. Cutter's 'Rules for a dictionary catalog', published in the United States in 1876, and the German-language 'Prussian Instructions' (1899), widely influential in Central Europe and German-speaking countries, are examples. Both the American and the British Library Associations (in 1879 and 1883 respectively) produced their own codes of rules.

In the early years of the twentieth century the two last-named Associations were individually contemplating revision of their respective sets of rules. The possibility of a joint code, representing, effectively, a standard code of cataloguing practice for the English-speaking world was proposed. The result was *Cataloguing rules: author and title entries*, published in 1908, and more frequently referred to as the 'A.A. (Anglo-American) Code', the '1908 Code', or the 'Joint Code'. This remained the basis for 'author' and descriptive cataloguing, in Britain at least, for almost 60 years.

Some tentative moves towards a joint revision of the '1908 Code' were made in the 1930s, but World War II intervened. The American Library Association went ahead alone with the revision: the outcome being the *A.L.A. Cataloguing Rules* published in 1949. This revision made little impact in Britain, but was critically received in the United States; chiefly because it represented a considerable increase in size and complexity over the '1908 Code'. One of the foremost critics was Seymour Lubetzky, whose views were trenchantly expressed in *Cataloguing rules and principles: a critique of the A.L.A. rules for entry and a proposed design for their revision*, published in 1953. The 'proposed design for their revision' was based upon the identification of broad, basic cataloguing problems (or bibliographic conditions, as Lubetzky called them) instead of upon an attempt to enumerate specific problems and situations (or cases), which had been the approach of all earlier codes of cataloguing rules.

The American Library Association then embarked upon a further revision of their rules, with Lubetzky's ideas as a basis. During this process the committees of the British and Canadian Library Associations which were concerned with rules revision, began to cooperate with their counterparts in the United States. Eventually, in 1967, the 'new' code appeared: now officially entitled *Anglo-American Cataloguing Rules*. Unfortunately, whilst there was a very considerable measure of transatlantic agreement, the 'Rules' appeared in two versions: a British and a North American text. An influential factor had been a Statement of Principles which had emerged from an international conference on cataloguing principles held in Paris in 1961. This set out various principles concerning catalogue construction, aimed at establishing international uniformity of practice in the making of catalogues and bibliographies.

Even before this first edition of AACR appeared the British and American Library Associations had made an agreement to jointly monitor the application of the new rules and to discuss (without necessarily agreeing upon) any possible amendments. Between 1969 and 1974 a number of changes were agreed and promulgated in amendment bulletins. The most significant change was the complete revision of Chapter 6 – the rules for the descriptive cataloguing of monographs – in order to establish conformity with the International Standard Bibliographic Description (Monographs). The latter was the first in a series of standards, prepared under the auspices of the International Federation of Library Associations and Institutions (IFLA), intended, as the name implies, to further international uniformity in the structure of records for library materials. The revision of Chapter 6 was published in 1974 as a replacement fascicule for the original chapter.

Then, in 1974, a tripartite agreement was made between representatives of Canada, the United Kingdom and the United States to embark upon a second edition of AACR. The delegates at the meeting represented both the library associations and the national libraries of the three countries. A Joint Steering Committee for Revision of AACR (JSCAACR) was set up to coordinate the work, and also various national revision committees were appointed in the three countries involved.

The decision to revise the code of practice, such a relatively short time after the publication of the first edition, was viewed with a certain amount of disquiet by some librarians. However, arguably unfortunately, the implications of revision do not seem to have been very fully considered in libraries until the work of revision was completed and the second edition published. Only since then has there been some concerted questioning as to whether this is an appropriate time to revise cataloguing practice, however theoretically desirable some of the changes might be. The decisions of the British Library, the Library of Congress, and the National Library of Canada to implement AACR2 for their centrally produced bibliographic records with effect from January 1981 obviously has had considerable significance for the increasing number of libraries which are heavily dependent upon central agencies for their cataloguing services.

It is not the intention to discuss the arguments for and against the adoption of AACR2 in this present context. Whatever the practical difficulties which it poses, the objectives underlying the new edition are, in principle, very justifiable. They are to:

(a) Reconcile the British and North American texts of AACR: not only in decisions but also in presentation and expression.

(b) Consolidate the amendments made since 1969.

(c) Incorporate the international standards which had emerged since 1967. In the main this relates to the various International Standard Bibliographic Descriptions referred to earlier.

(d) Introduce fuller and more integrated provision for non-book materials: the importance of which, in libraries, had increased rapidly since 1967.

(e) Provide for the machine processing of cataloguing data, which was just beginning to develop during the period when AACR1 was in preparation.

AACR2 was published at the end of 1978, after a considerably shorter gestation period than any of its direct predecessors. However, it should be recognized that AACR2 is *not* a new code: it is a revision of an existing corpus of rules.

Structure of AACR2

The basic structure of AACR2 is different from that of AACR1. In AACR1 the outline structure is:

Part I	Rules for entry and heading: the *choice* and *form of headings*.
Part II	Rules for the descriptive cataloguing of books and book-like materials.
Part III	Rules for the (mainly descriptive) cataloguing of non-book materials.

In AACR2 the outline structure is:

Part I Rules for description. These are set out in a general chapter which applies to all types of library material, supplemented by a series of chapters dealing with the description of particular forms of library materials.

Part II Rules for the establishment of headings: a single collection of rules which apply to all kinds of materials.

The details of the organization and application of Part I – the rules for description – are not the concern of the present text, and will not be considered in any further detail.

The outline of Part II is as follows:

Chapter 20 Introduction to Part II.
Chapter 21 Access points (i.e. decisions on *what* entries should be made for a document).
Chapters 22–5 Forms of headings. Namely:
 Chapter 22 For names of persons.
 Chapter 23 For geographic names when they appear in headings.
 Chapter 24 For names of corporate bodies – organizations, etc.
 Chapter 25 For uniform titles.
Chapter 26 References.

We may now proceed to page 11, to the beginning of the algorithms themselves.

Selective list of further readings

Ayres, F. H., 'Main entry: lynch pin or dodo', *Journal of librarianship*, **10** (3), Jul. 1978, 170–81.

Bakewell, K. G. B., *A manual of cataloguing practice*, Oxford, Pergamon Press, 1972, 1–13, 25–69.

Downing, Joel, 'Anniversary and birth: AA1908 to AACR2', *Library Association record*, **8** (2), Feb. 1979, 66–7.

Gorman, Michael, 'The Anglo-American Cataloguing Rules. Second edition', *Library resources and technical services*, **22** (3), Summer 1978, 209–25.

Hunter, Eric and Fox, Nicholas, *Examples illustrating AACR2*, London, Library Association, 1980.

Needham, C. D., *Organizing knowledge in libraries: an introduction to information retrieval*, 2nd rev. edn., London, Andre Deutsch, 11–88.

GENERAL INTRODUCTION
TO THE ALGORITHMS

The organization of the rules in Part II of AACR2 reflects the order in which decisions must be taken in the cataloguing process. The cataloguer must:

- Firstly determine what entries (or access points) it is desirable to provide for a document; including the decision on main entry heading if the cataloguing policy of the institution concerned is to make a distinction between 'main' and 'added' entries.
  These decisions are covered by Algorithm 1.

- Secondly, establish the *form* which the headings for those entries will take – whether the heading is the name of a person, the name of an organization, or a title.
  These decisions are covered by Algorithm 2.

Before beginning to work through the algorithms the following points should be carefully noted.

(1) The algorithms will occasionally refer to the 'chief source of information' for a document. This is the part of the document whence the data for cataloguing the item is normally drawn, e.g. the title page of a book. It is specified for each form of material at the beginning of each of the special chapters (2–12) in Part I of the Rules.

(2) The text of the algorithms will normally give a summary of the solution prescribed by the Rules. However, the algorithms should not be regarded as a substitute for the Rules themselves. It will usually be preferable to check the terms of the rules in AACR2 itself (where the examples provided will also be helpful): the appropriate rule numbers are signalled at decision points in the algorithm. In a few cases where the provisions of a ruling are too complex to be expressed in the algorithm you will simply be referred to the appropriate rule number.

(3) The algorithm sometimes indicates specifically the need to provide added entries under alternative access points or references from alternative headings, but generally this is only done when such provision is regarded as being particularly important. The student should be aware, in general, of the directions of the Rules with regard to added entries (Rules 21.29–21.30) and to references (Chapter 26): these are not covered directly by the algorithm.

(4) Some decisions may assume that the student is working in the context of a catalogue. e.g. on page 44, where you are asked to decide 'if there is likely to be confusion between this title and other titles entered under the same heading'. Alternatively, there may be decisions which would be determined by the cataloguing policy of the organization involved, e.g. on page 35 when you must decide whether or not to establish a uniform title. Obviously such decisions can be taken realistically if one is actually working in the context of a catalogue. Otherwise the student should ask the advice of a tutor or take an ad hoc decision.

(5) Occasionally the algorithm may contain an instruction to the effect of 'enter under the heading appropriate for the original work'. This means that you must return to an appropriate point in the algorithm in order to establish that 'appropriate heading'. Sometimes

there will be an indication in the algorithm when this is necessary, but there will be instances when the student must recognize the need to do so on his or her own account. *It is vital that the need to do this is recognized: the point being that there may be several levels or stages in the solving of a problem.*

(6) Make your decisions systematically by adhering strictly to the progression of the algorithm. Do not omit stages, and do not 'guess' your decisions.

(7) Do not be deterred by the apparent complexity of some of the pages: you are concerned in following only *one* of the strands on the flowchart.

(8) Make notes of your decisions as you go along. Firstly of the access points which you decide are necessary as you work through Algorithm 1, and then of the elements of headings as you establish them in progressing through Algorithm 2.

(9) Finally, it is important to be aware of the decisions that you are making, and that you do not merely follow the algorithm blindly.

ALGORITHM 1
ACCESS POINTS

A comparatively rare occurrence is that the title and/or author of a document may have changed, either between *editions* of the work or between *parts* of a work which is in more than one physical part. It is necessary, at the outset, to check this possibility.

NOTE

(1) A 'title proper' is defined by AACR2 as 'the chief name of an item, including any alternative title but excluding parallel titles and other title information'.

(2) In general, consider a title proper to have changed if any word other than an article, preposition or conjunction is added, deleted, or changed, or if the order of the first five words (first six words if the title begins with an article) is changed.

However, in general do not consider a title proper to have changed if:

(a) the change is in the representation of a word or words (e.g. abbreviated word or symbol vs. spelled out form; singular vs. plural form; one spelling vs. another).

(b) the addition, deletion or change comes after the first five words (the first six words if the title begins with an article) and does not change the meaning of the title or indicate a different subject matter.

(c) the only change is the addition or deletion of the name of the issuing body (and any grammatical connection) at the end of the title.

(d) the only change is in the addition, deletion, or change of punctuation.

In cases of doubt, consider the title proper to have changed. Rule 22.2A1.

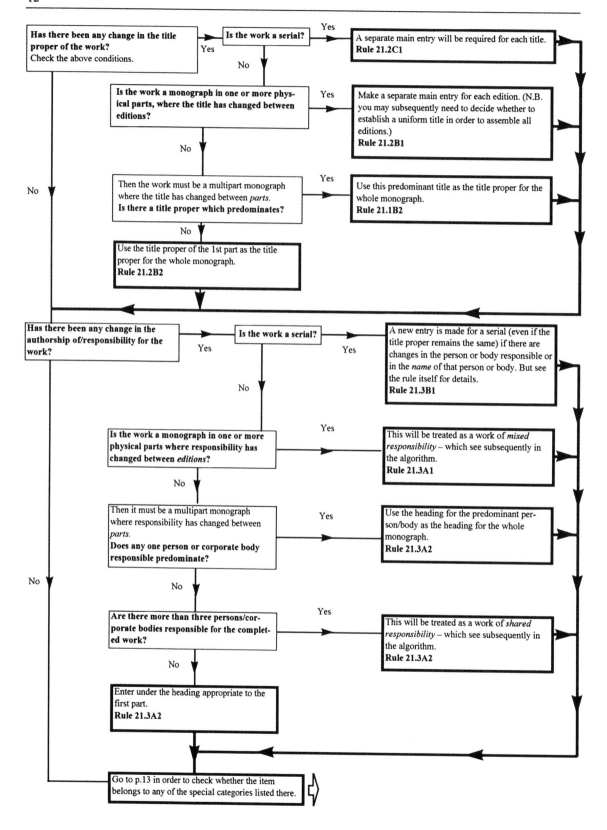

Has there been any change in the title proper of the work?
Check the above conditions.

Yes → **Is the work a serial?**

Yes → A separate main entry will be required for each title.
Rule 21.2C1

No ↓

Is the work a monograph in one or more physical parts, where the title has changed between editions?

Yes → Make a separate main entry for each edition. (N.B. you may subsequently need to decide whether to establish a uniform title in order to assemble all editions.)
Rule 21.2B1

No ↓

Then the work must be a multipart monograph where the title has changed between *parts*.
Is there a title proper which predominates?

Yes → Use this predominant title as the title proper for the whole monograph.
Rule 21.1B2

No ↓

Use the title proper of the 1st part as the title proper for the whole monograph.
Rule 21.2B2

No ↓ (left path)

Has there been any change in the authorship of/responsibility for the work?

Yes → **Is the work a serial?**

Yes → A new entry is made for a serial (even if the title proper remains the same) if there are changes in the person or body responsible or in the *name* of that person or body. But see the rule itself for details.
Rule 21.3B1

No ↓

Is the work a monograph in one or more physical parts where responsibility has changed between *editions*?

Yes → This will be treated as a work of *mixed responsibility* – which see subsequently in the algorithm.
Rule 21.3A1

No ↓

Then it must be a multipart monograph where responsibility has changed between *parts*.
Does any one person or corporate body responsible predominate?

Yes → Use the heading for the predominant person/body as the heading for the whole monograph.
Rule 21.3A2

No ↓

Are there more than three persons/corporate bodies responsible for the completed work?

Yes → This will be treated as a work of *shared responsibility* – which see subsequently in the algorithm.
Rule 21.3A2

No ↓

Enter under the heading appropriate to the first part.
Rule 21.3A2

No ↓ (left path)

Go to p.13 in order to check whether the item belongs to any of the special categories listed there.

The next question is to single out certain special categories of publications which present particular problems to the cataloguer:
(Note: serial publications are no longer treated as special categories.)

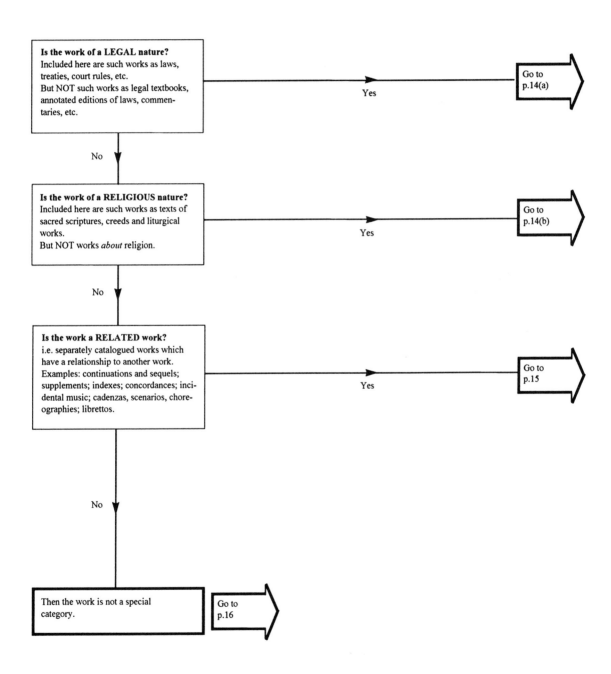

Is the work of a LEGAL nature?
Included here are such works as laws, treaties, court rules, etc.
But NOT such works as legal textbooks, annotated editions of laws, commentaries, etc.

Yes → Go to p.14(a)

No

Is the work of a RELIGIOUS nature?
Included here are such works as texts of sacred scriptures, creeds and liturgical works.
But NOT works *about* religion.

Yes → Go to p.14(b)

No

Is the work a RELATED work?
i.e. separately catalogued works which have a relationship to another work.
Examples: continuations and sequels; supplements; indexes; concordances; incidental music; cadenzas, scenarios, choreographies; librettos.

Yes → Go to p.15

No

Then the work is not a special category.

Go to p.16

(a) You have arrived here by deciding that:
    The work is of a LEGAL nature.

This category of document is NOT covered by the algorithm, as the decisions may be more conveniently made by referring directly to the rules. Select the appropriate heading below, and refer directly to the rule stated.

Laws	21.31
Administrative regulations	21.32
Constitutions and charters	21.33
Court rules	21.34
Treaties and intergovernmental agreement	21.35
Court decisions and cases	21.36

(b) You have arrived here by deciding that:
    The work is of a RELIGIOUS nature.

This category of document is NOT covered by the algorithm, as the decisions may be more conveniently made by referring directly to the rules. Select the appropriate heading below, and refer directly to the rule stated.

Sacred scriptures	21.37
Creeds and confessions of faith	21.38
Liturgical works	21.39

You have arrived here by deciding that:
The work is RELATED to another work.

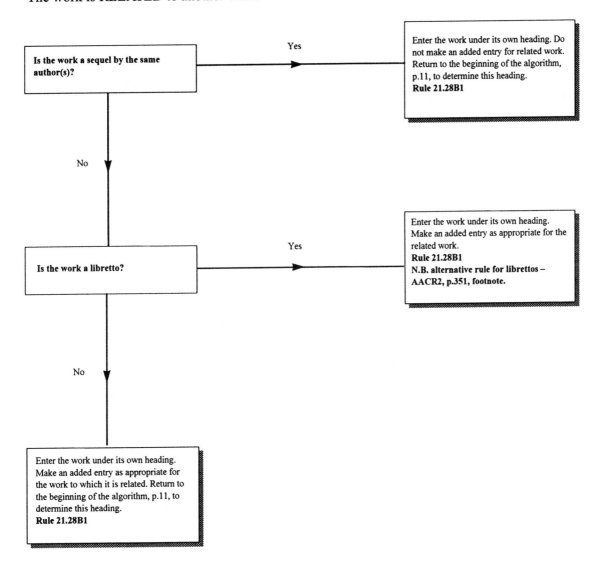

Is the work a sequel by the same author(s)?

Yes → Enter the work under its own heading. Do not make an added entry for related work. Return to the beginning of the algorithm, p.11, to determine this heading.
Rule 21.28B1

No ↓

Is the work a libretto?

Yes → Enter the work under its own heading. Make an added entry as appropriate for the related work.
Rule 21.28B1
N.B. alternative rule for librettos – AACR2, p.351, footnote.

No ↓

Enter the work under its own heading. Make an added entry as appropriate for the work to which it is related. Return to the beginning of the algorithm, p.11, to determine this heading.
Rule 21.28B1

As well as decisions dictated above, check if other added entries are required, e.g. under series. See Rules 21.29 and 21.30.

You have arrived here, having explored changes in author and/or title, and having decided that either:

(1) The work does not belong to the special categories listed on page 13
or
(2) The work is a related work and requires entry under its own heading.

You must now decide the nature of the authorship of the document, e.g. single authorship, unknown authorship, shared authorship, etc.

Before beginning to work through the algorithm, read the following notes carefully.

Two basic terms require definition:

Author (personal author) – the person chiefly responsible for the creation of the intellectual or artistic content of a work, e.g. writers of books, composers of music.

Corporate body – any organization or group of persons that is identified by a particular name and that acts, or may act, as an entity. Typical examples of corporate bodies are associations, institutions, business firms, non-profit enterprises, governments, government agencies, religious bodies, local churches and conferences.

In certain cases, corporate bodies may be regarded as being responsible for the creation of documents. In such cases the main entry will be made under the appropriate heading for the corporate body. This will apply if the document falls into one or more of the following categories:

(a) Those of an administrative nature dealing with the corporate body itself,
or its internal policies, procedures, finances, and/or operations
or its officers, staff and/or membership (e.g. directories)
or its resources (e.g. catalogues, inventories).

(b) Some legal, governmental and religious works. See Rule 21.1B2 for the list of types covered and refer to appropriate rules as directed.

(c) Those that record the collective thought of the body (e.g. reports of commissions, official statements on external policies).

(d) Those that report the collective activity of a conference (e.g. proceedings, collected papers), of an expedition (e.g. results of exploration, investigation), or of an event (e.g. an exhibition, fair, festival) falling within the definition of a corporate body (see definition – 21.1B1), provided that the conference, expedition, or event is prominently named in the item being catalogued.

(e) Those that result from the collective activity of a performing group as a whole where the responsibility of the group goes beyond that of mere performance, execution, etc. Publications resulting from such activity include sound recordings, films, videorecordings, and written records of performances. (See 21.23 for corporate bodies that function solely as performers on sound recordings.)

(f) Cartographic materials emanating from a corporate body other than a body that is merely responsible for their publication or distribution.

In case of doubt as to whether a work falls into one or more of these categories, treat it as if it does not.

Now select the appropriate authorship condition from below. Consider each carefully in the order in which they occur.

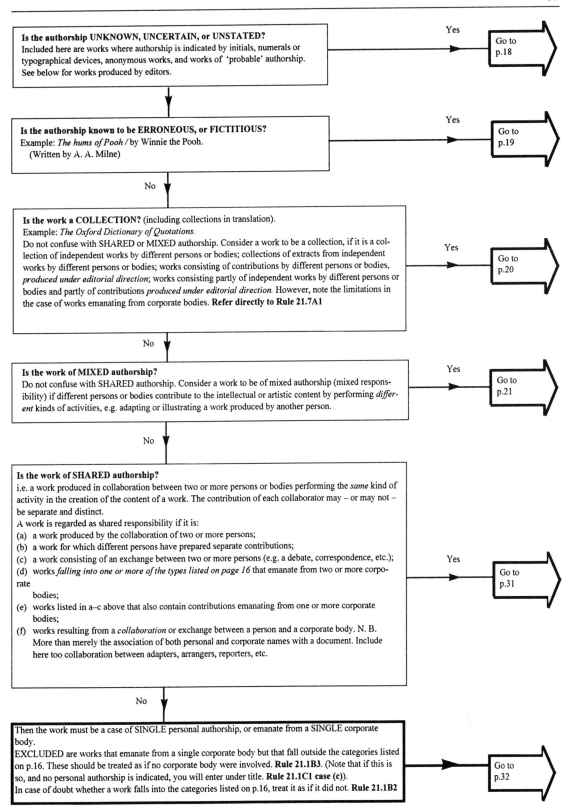

Is the authorship UNKNOWN, UNCERTAIN, or UNSTATED?
Included here are works where authorship is indicated by initials, numerals or typographical devices, anonymous works, and works of 'probable' authorship. See below for works produced by editors.

Yes → Go to p.18

Is the authorship known to be ERRONEOUS, or FICTITIOUS?
Example: *The hums of Pooh* / by Winnie the Pooh.
 (Written by A. A. Milne)

Yes → Go to p.19

No ↓

Is the work a COLLECTION? (including collections in translation).
Example: *The Oxford Dictionary of Quotations.*
Do not confuse with SHARED or MIXED authorship. Consider a work to be a collection, if it is a collection of independent works by different persons or bodies; collections of extracts from independent works by different persons or bodies; works consisting of contributions by different persons or bodies, *produced under editorial direction*; works consisting partly of independent works by different persons or bodies and partly of contributions *produced under editorial direction.* However, note the limitations in the case of works emanating from corporate bodies. **Refer directly to Rule 21.7A1**

Yes → Go to p.20

No ↓

Is the work of MIXED authorship?
Do not confuse with SHARED authorship. Consider a work to be of mixed authorship (mixed responsibility) if different persons or bodies contribute to the intellectual or artistic content by performing *different* kinds of activities, e.g. adapting or illustrating a work produced by another person.

Yes → Go to p.21

No ↓

Is the work of SHARED authorship?
i.e. a work produced in collaboration between two or more persons or bodies performing the *same* kind of activity in the creation of the content of a work. The contribution of each collaborator may – or may not – be separate and distinct.
A work is regarded as shared responsibility if it is:
(a) a work produced by the collaboration of two or more persons;
(b) a work for which different persons have prepared separate contributions;
(c) a work consisting of an exchange between two or more persons (e.g. a debate, correspondence, etc.);
(d) works *falling into one or more of the types listed on page 16* that emanate from two or more corporate
  bodies;
(e) works listed in a–c above that also contain contributions emanating from one or more corporate
  bodies;
(f) works resulting from a *collaboration* or exchange between a person and a corporate body. N. B.
  More than merely the association of both personal and corporate names with a document. Include
  here too collaboration between adapters, arrangers, reporters, etc.

Yes → Go to p.31

No ↓

Then the work must be a case of SINGLE personal authorship, or emanate from a SINGLE corporate body.
EXCLUDED are works that emanate from a single corporate body but that fall outside the categories listed on p.16. These should be treated as if no corporate body were involved. **Rule 21.1B3.** (Note that if this is so, and no personal authorship is indicated, you will enter under title. **Rule 21.1C1 case (c)**).
In case of doubt whether a work falls into the categories listed on p.16, treat it as if it did not. **Rule 21.1B2**

Go to p.32

You have arrived here by deciding that:
The work is of UNKNOWN, UNCERTAIN or UNSTATED authorship.

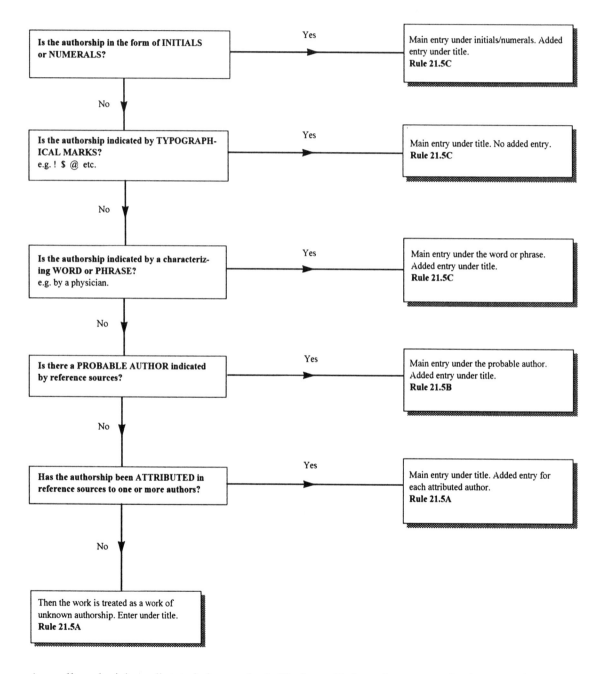

As well as decisions dictated above, check if other added entries are required, e.g. under series.
See Rules 21.29 and 21.30.

You have arrived here by deciding that:
The work is of ERRONEOUS or FICTITIOUS authorship.

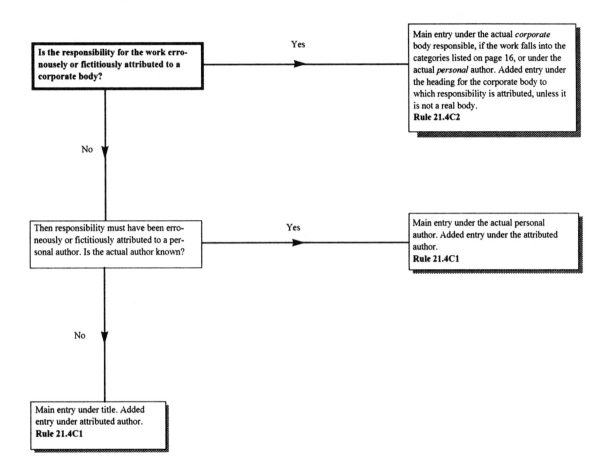

As well as decisions dictated above, check if other added entries are required, e.g. under series. See Rules 21.29 and 21.30.

You have arrived here by deciding that:
The work is a COLLECTION.

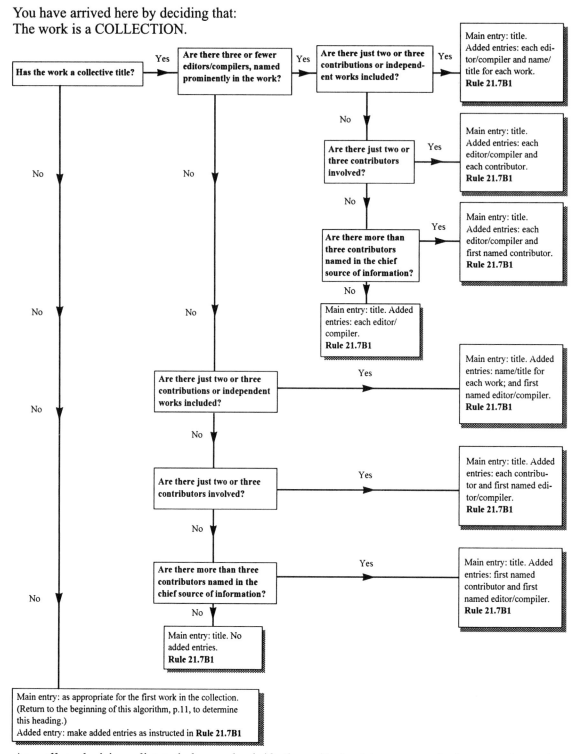

As well as decisions dictated above, check if other added entries are required, e.g. under series. See Rules 21.29 and 21.30.

You have arrived here by deciding that:
The authorship is MIXED responsibility.

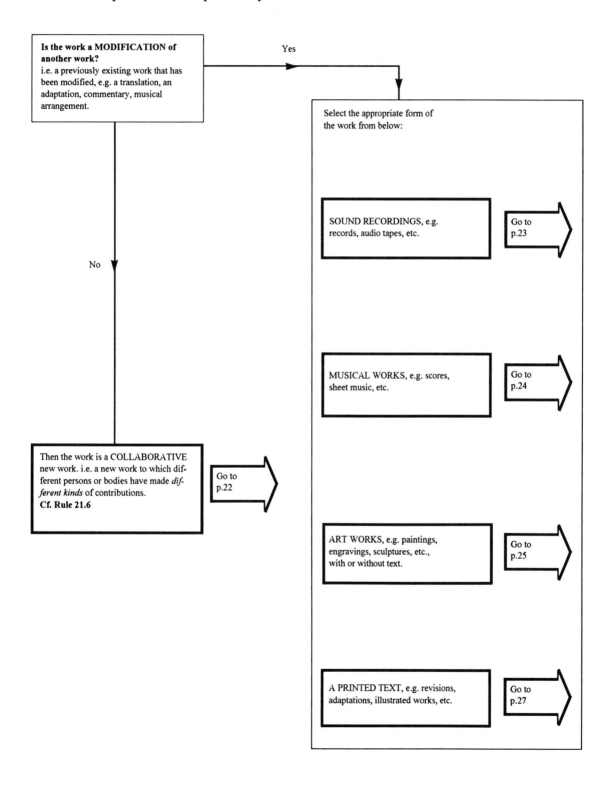

Is the work a MODIFICATION of another work?
i.e. a previously existing work that has been modified, e.g. a translation, an adaptation, commentary, musical arrangement.

Yes

No

Then the work is a COLLABORATIVE new work. i.e. a new work to which different persons or bodies have made *different kinds* of contributions.
Cf. Rule 21.6

Go to p.22

Select the appropriate form of the work from below:

SOUND RECORDINGS, e.g. records, audio tapes, etc.

Go to p.23

MUSICAL WORKS, e.g. scores, sheet music, etc.

Go to p.24

ART WORKS, e.g. paintings, engravings, sculptures, etc., with or without text.

Go to p.25

A PRINTED TEXT, e.g. revisions, adaptations, illustrated works, etc.

Go to p.27

You have arrived here by deciding that:
The work is a COLLABORATIVE new work. (N.B. AACR2 treats works consisting of words and music as modifications of existing works: see page 27.).

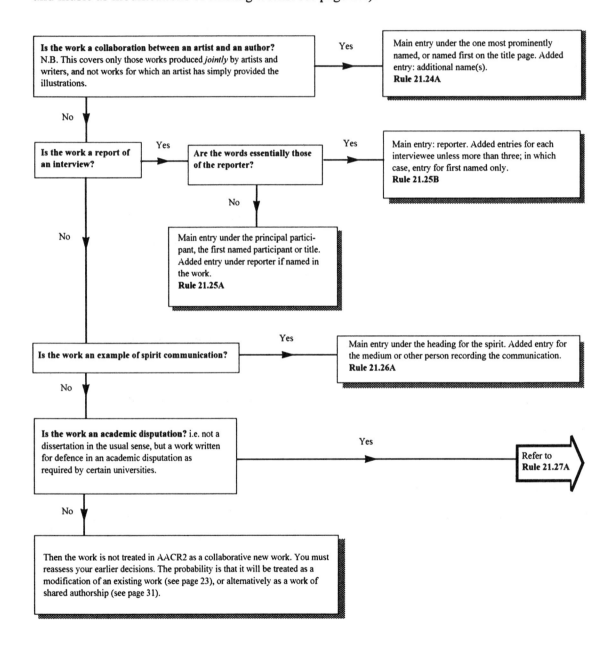

As well as decisions dictated above, check if other added entries are required, e.g. under series. See Rules 21.29 and 21.30.

You have arrived here by deciding that:
The authorship is MIXED RESPONSIBILITY and the work is a MODIFICATION of an existing work in the form of a SOUND RECORDING.

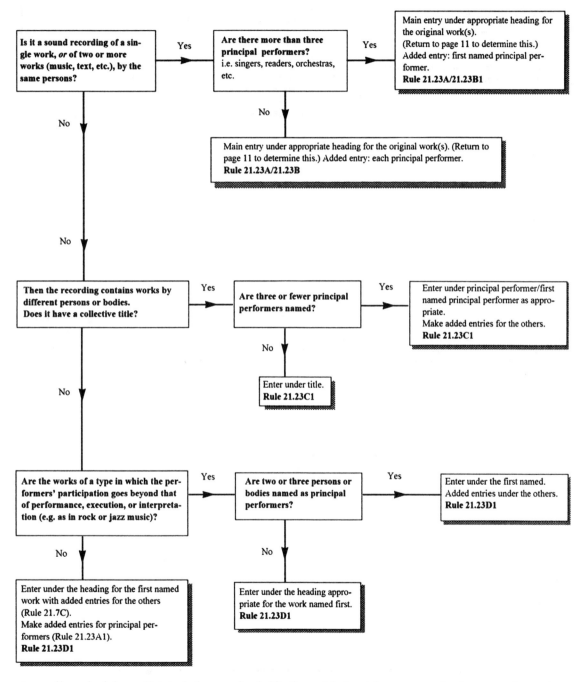

As well as decisions dictated above, check if other added entries are required, e.g. under series. See Rules 21.29 and 21.30.

You have arrived here by deciding that:
The authorship is MIXED RESPONSIBILITY and the work is a MODIFICATION of an existing work in the form of a MUSICAL WORK.

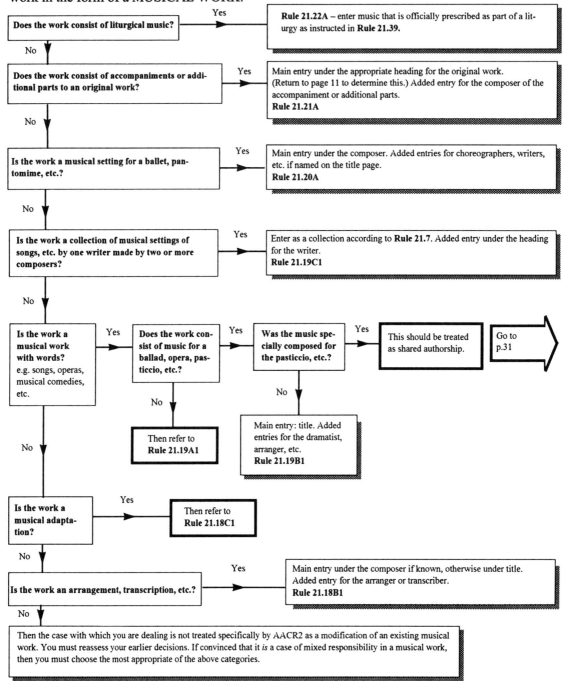

As well as decisions dictated above, check if other added entries are required, e.g. under series. See Rules 21.29 and 21.30.

You have arrived here by deciding that:
The authorship is MIXED RESPONSIBILITY and the work is a MODIFICATION of an existing work in the form of an ART WORK.
(N.B. Collections of works by *different* artists will be treated *as* collections. See page 20).

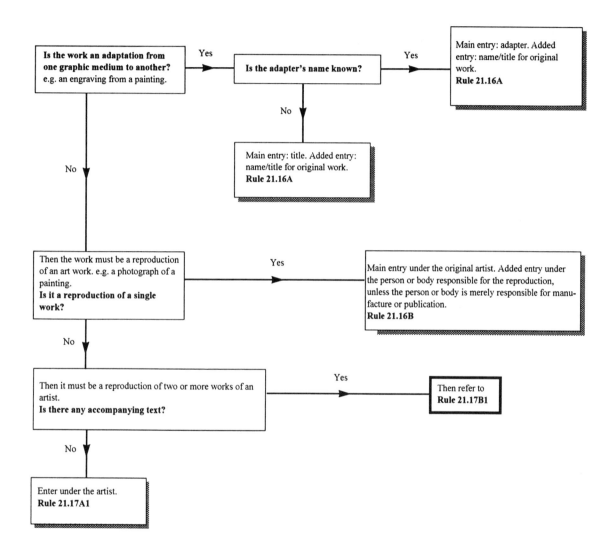

As well as decisions dictated above, check if other added entries are required, e.g. under series. See Rules 21.29 and 21.30.

You have arrived here by deciding that:
The work is of MIXED RESPONSIBILITY and is a MODIFICATION of an existing work in the form of an ILLUSTRATED TEXT.

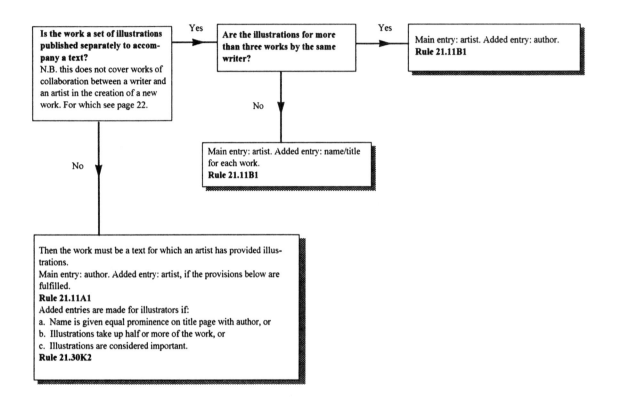

As well as decisions dictated above, check if other added entries are required, e.g. under series. See Rules 21.29 and 21.30.

You have arrived here by deciding that:
The work is of MIXED RESPONSIBILITY and is a MODIFICATION of an existing work in the form of a PRINTED TEXT.
Select from below:

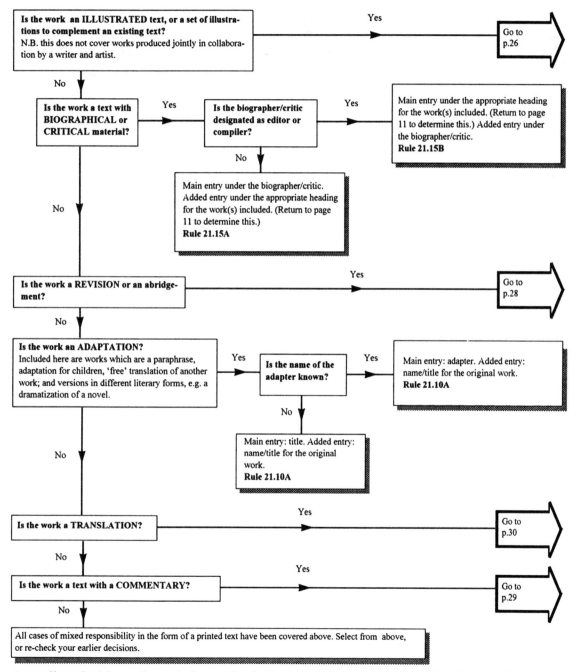

As well as decisions dictated above, check if other added entries are required, e.g. under series. See Rules 21.29 and 21.30.

You have arrived here by deciding that:
The work is of MIXED RESPONSIBILITY and is a MODIFICATION of an existing work in the form of a REVISED TEXT.

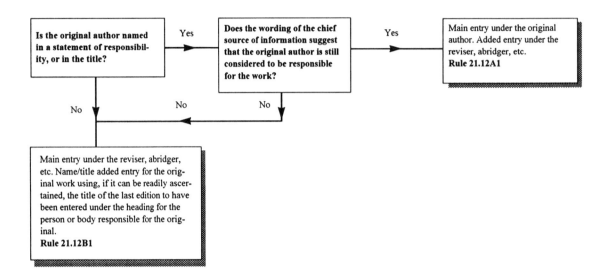

As well as decisions dictated above, check if other added entries are required, e.g. under series. See Rules 21.29 and 21.30.

You have arrived here by deciding that:
The work is of MIXED RESPONSIBILITY and is a MODIFICATION of an existing work in the form of a TEXT with COMMENTARY.

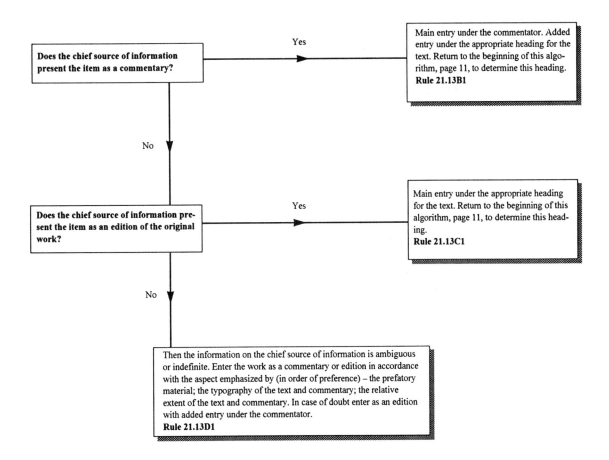

As well as decisions dictated above, check if other added entries are required, e.g. under series. See Rules 21.29 and 21.30.

You have arrived here by deciding that:

The work is of MIXED RESPONSIBILITY and is a MODIFICATION of an existing work in the form of a TRANSLATED TEXT.

Main entry under the appropriate heading for the original work.
Return to the beginning of this algorithm, page 11, to determine this heading.
Added entry under the translator if the provisions below are fulfilled.
Rule 21.14A

Added entry is made for the translator if the main entry heading is for a corporate body or under title. When the main entry is a personal author, an added entry is made for the translator if:

(a) The translation is in verse, or
(b) Important in its own right, or
(c) The work has been translated into the same language more than once, or
(d) The wording of the chief source of information suggests the translator is the author, or
(e) The main entry heading may be difficult for readers to find (e.g. as with oriental or mediaeval works).

Rule 21.30K1

As well as decisions dictated above, check if other added entries are required, e.g. under series. See Rules 21.29 and 21.30.

You have arrived here by deciding that:
The work is of SHARED RESPONSIBILITY.

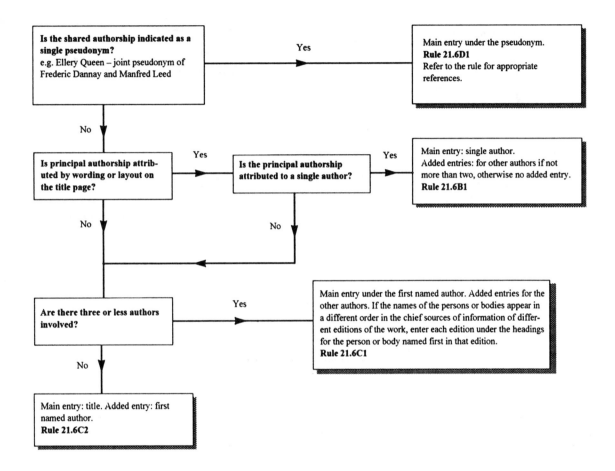

As well as decisions dictated above, check if other entries are required, e.g. under series. See Rules 21.29 and 21.30.

You have arrived here by deciding that:
The work is of SINGLE personal authorship, or emanates from a SINGLE corporate body.

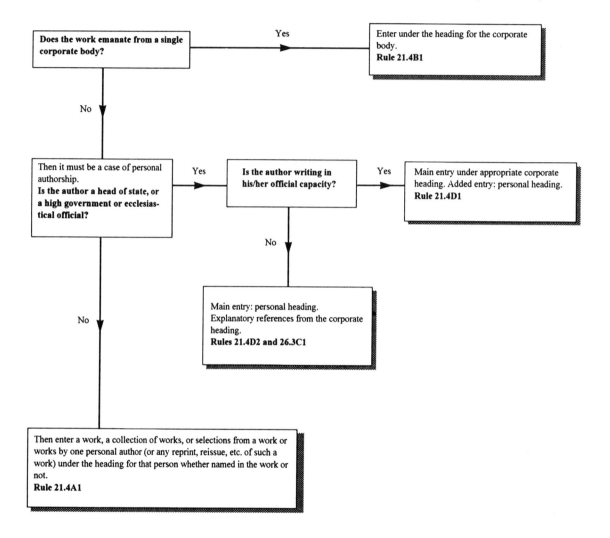

As well as decisions dictated above, check if other added entries are required, e.g. under series. See Rules 21.29 and 21.30.

ALGORITHM 2
FORM OF HEADING

You have decided upon the entries or access points required for a document. It will now be necessary to determine the *form* which the headings for these entries will take. There will be a main entry and, usually, a number of added entries. It may also be necessary to provide references from discounted forms of headings to the preferred forms. e.g. A main entry under the name of a personal author, with added entries under the name of a corporate body in some way associated with the document and under its title. Consequently you may need to check, ultimately, more than one of the following strands.

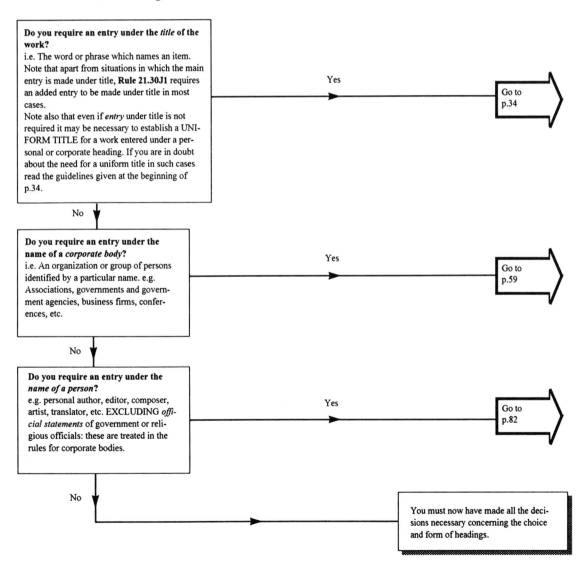

Do you require an entry under the *title* of the work?
i.e. The word or phrase which names an item. Note that apart from situations in which the main entry is made under title, **Rule 21.30J1** requires an added entry to be made under title in most cases.
Note also that even if *entry* under title is not required it may be necessary to establish a UNIFORM TITLE for a work entered under a personal or corporate heading. If you are in doubt about the need for a uniform title in such cases read the guidelines given at the beginning of p.34.

Yes → Go to p.34

No ↓

Do you require an entry under the name of a *corporate body*?
i.e. An organization or group of persons identified by a particular name. e.g. Associations, governments and government agencies, business firms, conferences, etc.

Yes → Go to p.59

No ↓

Do you require an entry under the *name of a person*?
e.g. personal author, editor, composer, artist, translator, etc. EXCLUDING *official statements* of government or religious officials: these are treated in the rules for corporate bodies.

Yes → Go to p.82

No ↓

You must now have made all the decisions necessary concerning the choice and form of headings.

You have arrived here by deciding that an entry under TITLE is required.

If the work being catalogued has appeared at different times under varying titles then it may be necessary to establish a UNIFORM TITLE. i.e. a particular title by which the work may be identified for cataloguing purposes in order to collocate, or bring together, all entries for a particular work under that one form of title rather than distribute entries for that work under a number (possibly a very large number) of different titles. An example would be *The Arabian nights*, which has appeared under very many variant titles in its different editions and versions.

Even if a work is entered under the heading of a personal author or corporate body it may be considered necessary to establish a uniform title.

> e.g. Defoe, Daniel
>   The life and adventures of Robinson Crusoe . . .
>
> Defoe, Daniel
>   The adventures of Robinson Crusoe . . .

These entries might be separated in a sequence of entries under the heading for Defoe.

If a uniform title, say, 'Robinson Crusoe' was to be established it would appear before the title proper in the catalogue entry, and thus collocate entries for the work 'Robinson Crusoe' under the heading for Defoe.

> i.e. Defoe, Daniel
>   [Robinson Crusoe]
>   The life and adventures of Robinson Crusoe . . .
>
> Defoe, Daniel
>   [Robinson Crusoe]
>   The adventures of Robinson Crusoe . . .

Consequently, Chapter 25 of AACR2 – Uniform titles – to which this section of the algorithm relates, considers the creation of uniform titles which may be used as headings *and/or* filing titles under an author heading.

Basic rules for uniform titles

(1) Uniform titles are normally given in square brackets, whether they appear as headings or otherwise.

(2) Titles selected as uniform titles which are in a non-roman script are transliterated according to the transliteration table for the language adopted by the cataloguing agency.

(3) If the main entry for a work is made under a uniform title then an added entry is made under the title proper for the work being catalogued, with references from any other variants of the title.

(4) If the main entry has been made under a personal author or corporate body and a uniform title is used then a name-title reference is made from variants of the title, with an added entry under the title proper of the work being catalogued. Read Rules 25.1–25.2 for further explanation.

AACR2 recognizes that the need to establish uniform titles may vary from one catalogue to another. In Rule 25.1A guidelines are laid down to assist in determining whether a uniform title should be established. These are:

(1) How well the work is known

(2) How many manifestations of the work are involved

(3) Whether the main entry is under title

(4) Whether the work was originally in another language

(5) The extent to which the catalogue is used for research purposes.

Rule 25.1A goes on to say, 'Although the rules in this chapter are stated as instructions, apply them according to the policy of the cataloguing agency'.

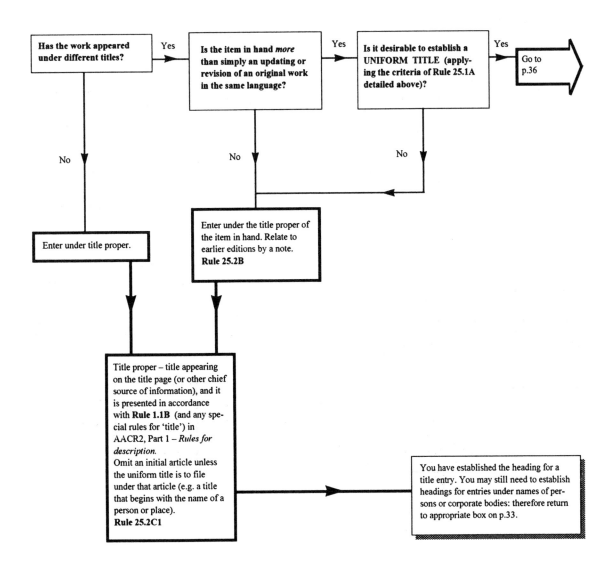

You have arrived here by deciding that:
an entry under TITLE is required and that a UNIFORM TITLE SHOULD BE ESTABLISHED.

Uniform titles for certain categories of works require special consideration. Note that more than one of the categories identified below might apply simultaneously in some instances. e.g. one might have a *liturgical work* which is also an *incunabulum,* or a *manuscript group* of *sacred scriptures*. The Rules themselves are not explicit as to the priority which should apply in situations such as these. Our decision has been to impose an order of precedence which follows the order in which the categories are listed below.

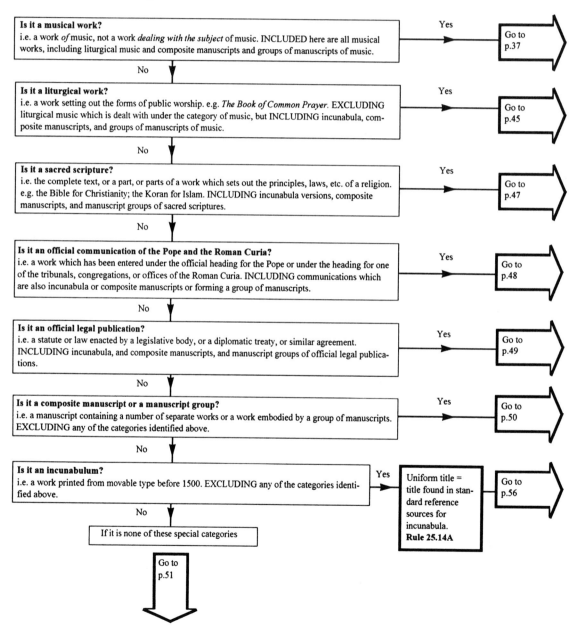

Is it a musical work?
i.e. a work *of* music, not a work *dealing with the subject* of music. INCLUDED here are all musical works, including liturgical music and composite manuscripts and groups of manuscripts of music.

Yes → Go to p.37

No ↓

Is it a liturgical work?
i.e. a work setting out the forms of public worship. e.g. *The Book of Common Prayer.* EXCLUDING liturgical music which is dealt with under the category of music, but INCLUDING incunabula, composite manuscripts, and groups of manuscripts of music.

Yes → Go to p.45

No ↓

Is it a sacred scripture?
i.e. the complete text, or a part, or parts of a work which sets out the principles, laws, etc. of a religion. e.g. the Bible for Christianity; the Koran for Islam. INCLUDING incunabula versions, composite manuscripts, and manuscript groups of sacred scriptures.

Yes → Go to p.47

No ↓

Is it an official communication of the Pope and the Roman Curia?
i.e. a work which has been entered under the official heading for the Pope or under the heading for one of the tribunals, congregations, or offices of the Roman Curia. INCLUDING communications which are also incunabula or composite manuscripts or forming a group of manuscripts.

Yes → Go to p.48

No ↓

Is it an official legal publication?
i.e. a statute or law enacted by a legislative body, or a diplomatic treaty, or similar agreement. INCLUDING incunabula, and composite manuscripts, and manuscript groups of official legal publications.

Yes → Go to p.49

No ↓

Is it a composite manuscript or a manuscript group?
i.e. a manuscript containing a number of separate works or a work embodied by a group of manuscripts. EXCLUDING any of the categories identified above.

Yes → Go to p.50

No ↓

Is it an incunabulum?
i.e. a work printed from movable type before 1500. EXCLUDING any of the categories identified above.

Yes → Uniform title = title found in standard reference sources for incunabula. **Rule 25.14A** → Go to p.56

No ↓

If it is none of these special categories

Go to p.51

You have arrived here by deciding that:
An entry under TITLE is required, a UNIFORM TITLE should be established and that you are dealing with a MUSICAL WORK (as defined on page 36).

You should begin by examining the definitions of 'Title' and 'Work' as given in the glossary (appendix D) of the code.

When determining the initial title element, omit the following:

(1) A statement of medium of performance

(2) Key

(3) Serial, opus, or thematic index numbers

(4) Number(s) (unless they are an integral part of the title)

(5) Date of composition

(6) Adjectives and epithets not part of the original title

(7) An initial article.

Rule 25.28A

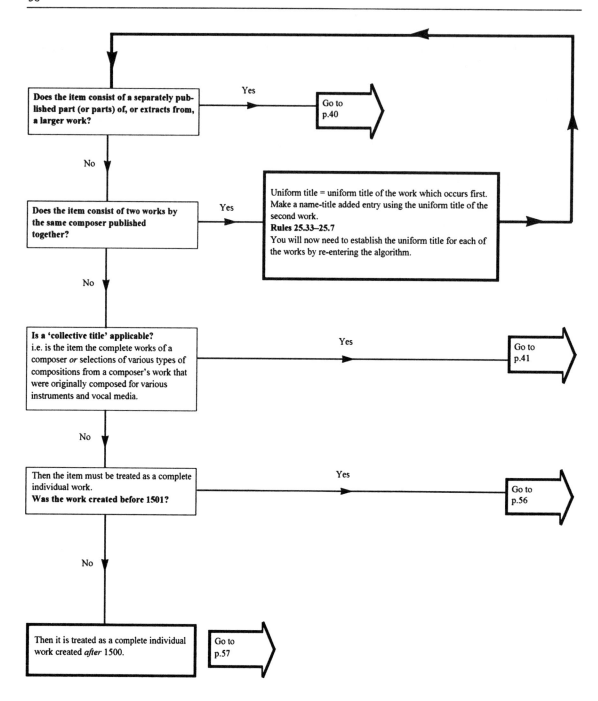

Does the item consist of a separately published part (or parts) of, or extracts from, a larger work?

Yes → Go to p.40

No ↓

Does the item consist of two works by the same composer published together?

Yes → Uniform title = uniform title of the work which occurs first. Make a name-title added entry using the uniform title of the second work.
Rules 25.33–25.7
You will now need to establish the uniform title for each of the works by re-entering the algorithm.

No ↓

Is a 'collective title' applicable?
i.e. is the item the complete works of a composer *or* selections of various types of compositions from a composer's work that were originally composed for various instruments and vocal media.

Yes → Go to p.41

No ↓

Then the item must be treated as a complete individual work.
Was the work created before 1501?

Yes → Go to p.56

No ↓

Then it is treated as a complete individual work created *after* 1500.

Go to p.57

You have arrived here by deciding that:
An entry under TITLE is required, a UNIFORM TITLE should be established and that an INDI-VIDUAL MUSICAL WORK is involved. In addition you have established the BASIS for the uniform title. The precise uniform title must now be formulated by applying Rules 25.27–25.35 to this basis.

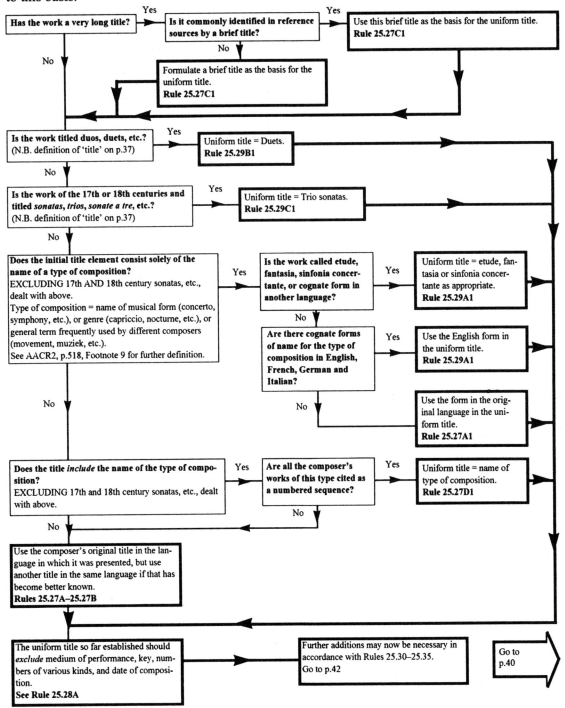

Go to p.40

Go to p.42

You have arrived here by deciding that:
An entry under TITLE is required, a UNIFORM TITLE should be established and that a PART or PARTS of, or EXTRACTS from, a MUSICAL WORK are involved.

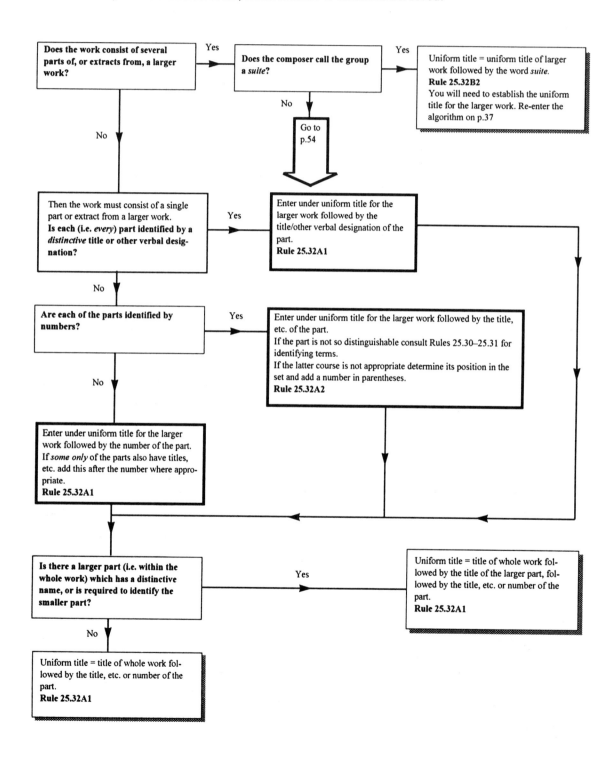

Does the work consist of several parts of, or extracts from, a larger work? — Yes →

Does the composer call the group a *suite*? — Yes →

Uniform title = uniform title of larger work followed by the word *suite*.
Rule 25.32B2
You will need to establish the uniform title for the larger work. Re-enter the algorithm on p.37

No ↓

Go to p.54

No ↓

Then the work must consist of a single part or extract from a larger work.
Is each (i.e. *every*) part identified by a *distinctive* title or other verbal designation? — Yes →

Enter under uniform title for the larger work followed by the title/other verbal designation of the part.
Rule 25.32A1

No ↓

Are each of the parts identified by numbers? — Yes →

Enter under uniform title for the larger work followed by the title, etc. of the part.
If the part is not so distinguishable consult Rules 25.30–25.31 for identifying terms.
If the latter course is not appropriate determine its position in the set and add a number in parentheses.
Rule 25.32A2

No ↓

Enter under uniform title for the larger work followed by the number of the part.
If *some only* of the parts also have titles, etc. add this after the number where appropriate.
Rule 25.32A1

Is there a larger part (i.e. within the whole work) which has a distinctive name, or is required to identify the smaller part? — Yes →

Uniform title = title of whole work followed by the title of the larger part, followed by the title, etc. or number of the part.
Rule 25.32A1

No ↓

Uniform title = title of whole work followed by the title, etc. or number of the part.
Rule 25.32A1

You have arrived here by deciding that:
An entry under TITLE is required, a UNIFORM TITLE should be established, you are dealing with a MUSICAL WORK, and that a COLLECTIVE TITLE (as defined on page 37) is applicable.

Definitions   As a preliminary it is necessary to define the way in which two terms are used in the Rules.

(1) *Type of composition* implies name of musical form (concerto, symphony, etc.) or genre (capriccio, nocturne, etc.), or a general term used frequently by different composers (movement, muziek, etc.). See AACR2, p.518, Footnote 9 for further definition.

(2) *Medium* means medium of performance, both instrumental and vocal. See AACR2, p.522, Footnote 10 for further definition.

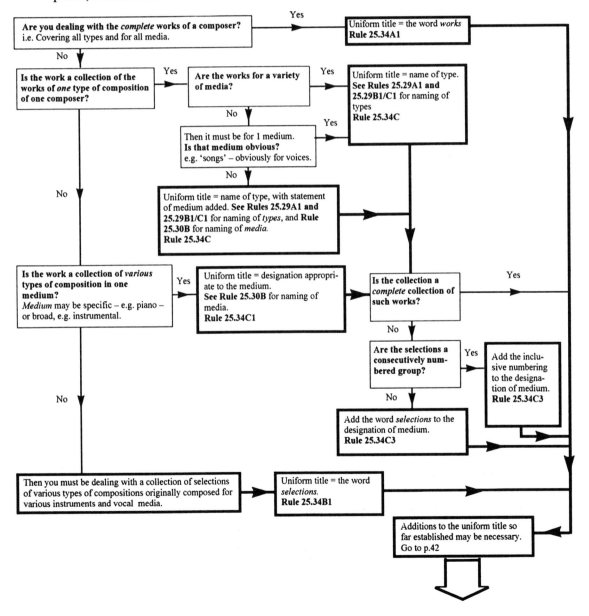

You have arrived here by deciding that:
An entry under TITLE is required, a UNIFORM TITLE should be established and that a MUSICAL WORK is involved. You have formulated a basic uniform title and must now decide what ADDITIONS to this title, if any, are necessary.

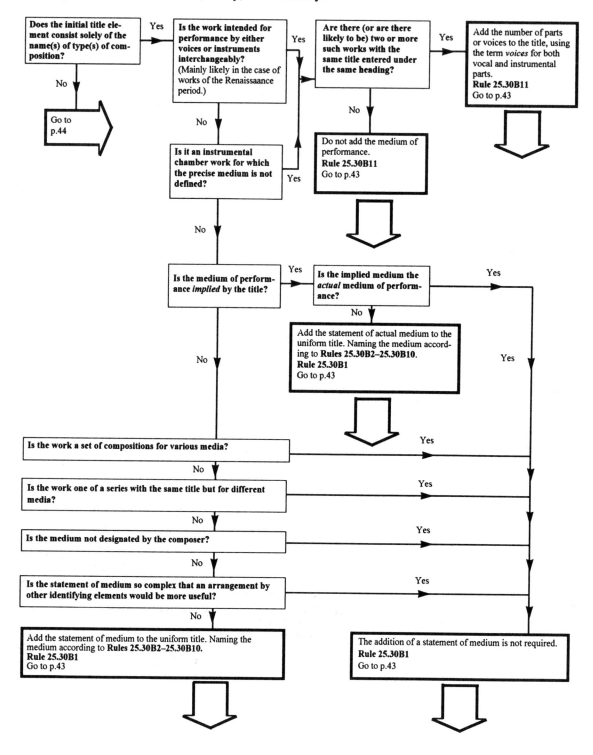

We are continuing with ADDITIONS to uniform titles for a MUSICAL WORK whose title is SOLELY THE NAME(S) OF A TYPE(S) OF COMPOSITION. You have taken a decision about the addition of medium of performance. You now need to decide about further additions. Any further additions appear in the uniform title in the order in which they occur below.

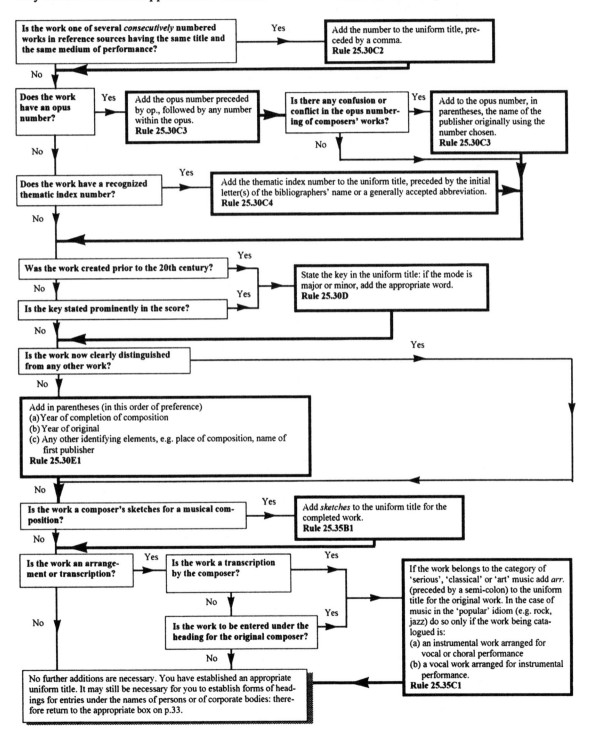

You have arrived here having established a UNIFORM TITLE for a MUSICAL WORK and now need to make decisions about ADDITIONS to the uniform title which consists of MORE than solely the name of a type of composition.

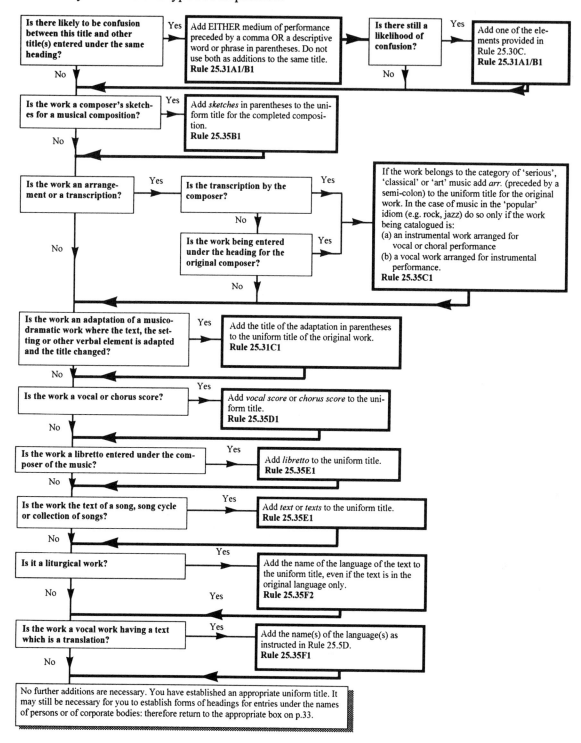

No further additions are necessary. You have established an appropriate uniform title. It may still be necessary for you to establish forms of headings for entries under the names of persons or of corporate bodies: therefore return to the appropriate box on p.33.

You have arrived here by deciding that:
An entry under TITLE is required, a UNIFORM TITLE should be established and that a
LITURGICAL WORK is involved.

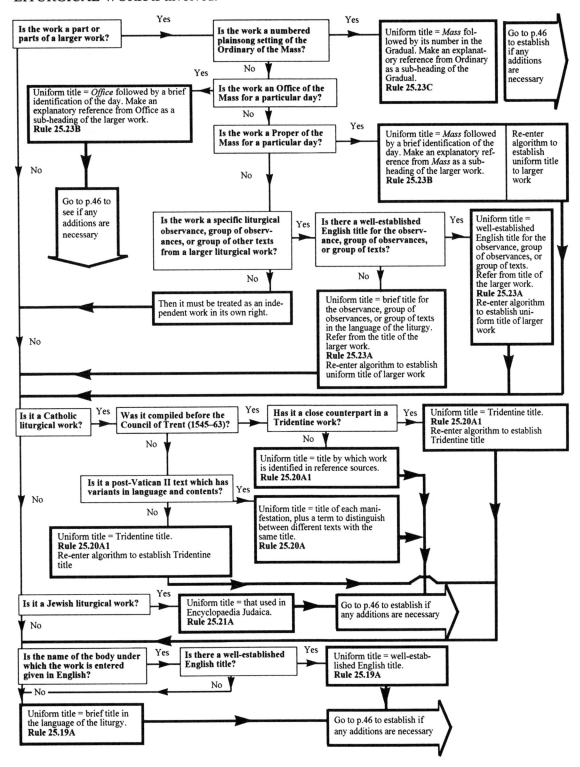

You have established a basic UNIFORM TITLE for a LITURGICAL WORK.
You now need to determine if any ADDITIONS to this basic title are necessary.

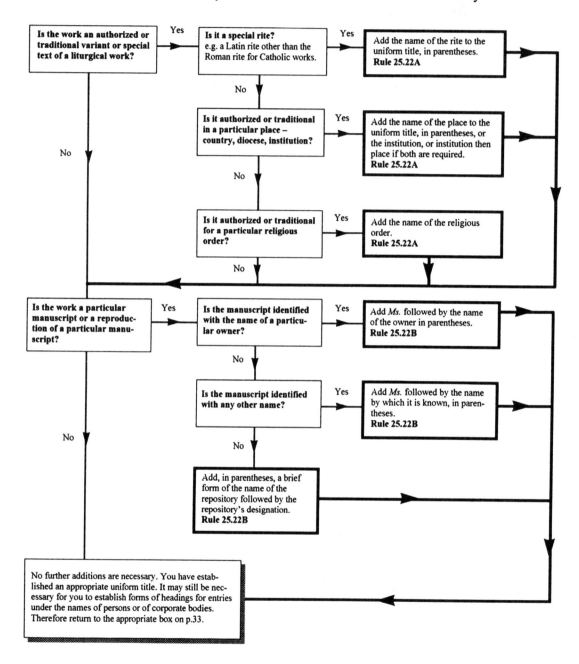

Is the work an authorized or traditional variant or special text of a liturgical work? — Yes → **Is it a special rite?** e.g. a Latin rite other than the Roman rite for Catholic works. — Yes → Add the name of the rite to the uniform title, in parentheses. **Rule 25.22A**

No ↓

Is it authorized or traditional in a particular place – country, diocese, institution? — Yes → Add the name of the place to the uniform title, in parentheses, or the institution, or institution then place if both are required. **Rule 25.22A**

No ↓

Is it authorized or traditional for a particular religious order? — Yes → Add the name of the religious order. **Rule 25.22A**

No

Is the work a particular manuscript or a reproduction of a particular manuscript? — Yes → **Is the manuscript identified with the name of a particular owner?** — Yes → Add *Ms.* followed by the name of the owner in parentheses. **Rule 25.22B**

No ↓

Is the manuscript identified with any other name? — Yes → Add *Ms.* followed by the name by which it is known, in parentheses. **Rule 25.22B**

No ↓

Add, in parentheses, a brief form of the name of the repository followed by the repository's designation. **Rule 25.22B**

No further additions are necessary. You have established an appropriate uniform title. It may still be necessary for you to establish forms of headings for entries under the names of persons or of corporate bodies. Therefore return to the appropriate box on p.33.

You have arrived here by deciding that:
An entry under TITLE is required, a UNIFORM TITLE should be established and that the work is the COMPLETE TEXT, a PART, or PARTS of a SACRED SCRIPTURE.

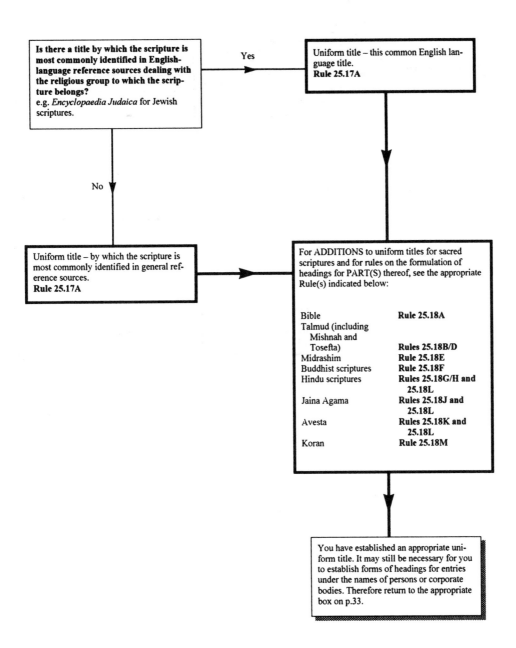

You have arrived here by deciding that:
An entry under TITLE is required, a UNIFORM TITLE should be established and that the work is an OFFICIAL PAPAL COMMUNICATION.

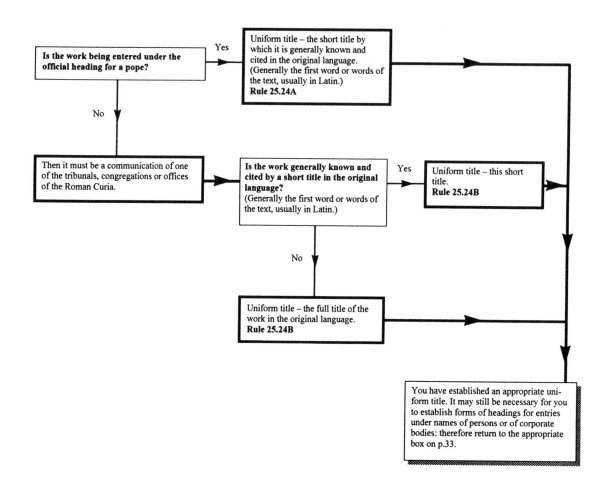

Is the work being entered under the official heading for a pope?

Yes → Uniform title – the short title by which it is generally known and cited in the original language. (Generally the first word or words of the text, usually in Latin.) **Rule 25.24A**

No ↓

Then it must be a communication of one of the tribunals, congregations or offices of the Roman Curia.

Is the work generally known and cited by a short title in the original language? (Generally the first word or words of the text, usually in Latin.)

Yes → Uniform title – this short title. **Rule 25.24B**

No ↓

Uniform title – the full title of the work in the original language. **Rule 25.24B**

You have established an appropriate uniform title. It may still be necessary for you to establish forms of headings for entries under names of persons or of corporate bodies: therefore return to the appropriate box on p.33.

You have arrived here by deciding that:
An entry under TITLE is required, a UNIFORM TITLE should be established and that the work is an OFFICIAL LEGAL PUBLICATION.

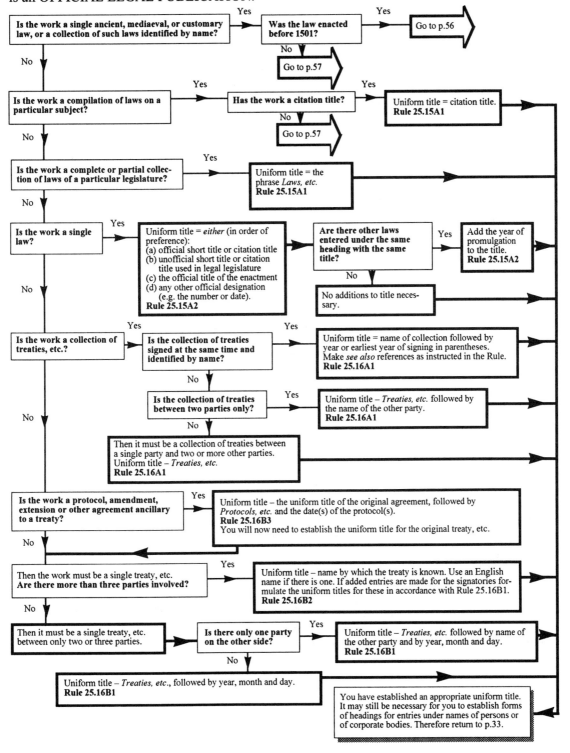

You have arrived here by deciding that:
An entry under TITLE is required, a UNIFORM TITLE should be established and that the work is a COMPOSITE MANUSCRIPT or MANUSCRIPT GROUP

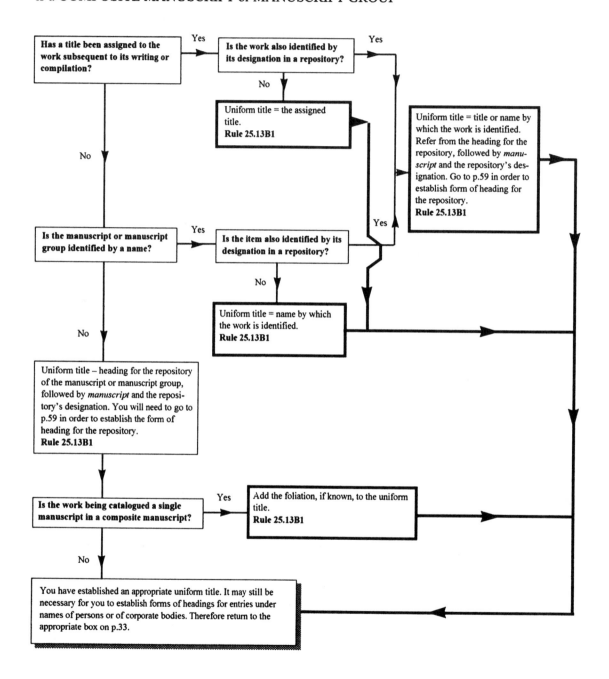

Has a title been assigned to the work subsequent to its writing or compilation?

Yes → Is the work also identified by its designation in a repository?

No ↓

Uniform title = the assigned title.
Rule 25.13B1

Yes →

Uniform title = title or name by which the work is identified. Refer from the heading for the repository, followed by *manuscript* and the repository's designation. Go to p.59 in order to establish form of heading for the repository.
Rule 25.13B1

No ↓

Is the manuscript or manuscript group identified by a name?

Yes → Is the item also identified by its designation in a repository?

No ↓

Uniform title = name by which the work is identified.
Rule 25.13B1

Yes ↑

No ↓

Uniform title – heading for the repository of the manuscript or manuscript group, followed by *manuscript* and the repository's designation. You will need to go to p.59 in order to establish the form of heading for the repository.
Rule 25.13B1

↓

Is the work being catalogued a single manuscript in a composite manuscript?

Yes → Add the foliation, if known, to the uniform title.
Rule 25.13B1

No ↓

You have established an appropriate uniform title. It may still be necessary for you to establish forms of headings for entries under names of persons or of corporate bodies. Therefore return to the appropriate box on p.33.

You have arrived here by deciding that:
An entry under TITLE is required, that a UNIFORM TITLE should be established and that the work does not fall into any of the special categories listed on page 36.

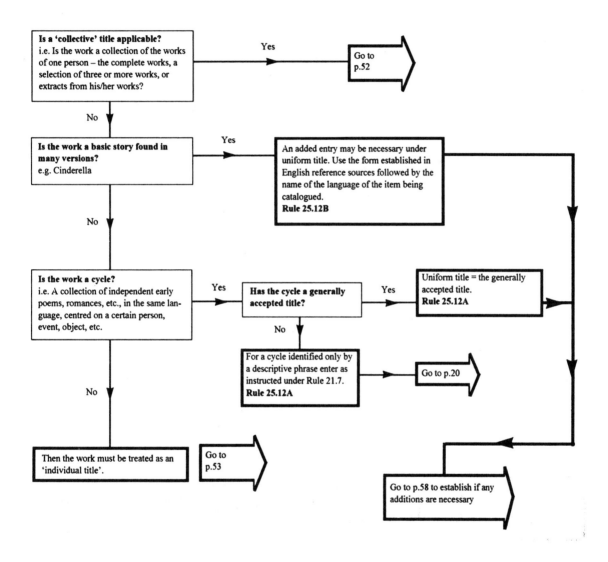

Is a 'collective' title applicable?
i.e. Is the work a collection of the works of one person – the complete works, a selection of three or more works, or extracts from his/her works?

Yes → Go to p.52

No ↓

Is the work a basic story found in many versions?
e.g. Cinderella

Yes → An added entry may be necessary under uniform title. Use the form established in English reference sources followed by the name of the language of the item being catalogued.
Rule 25.12B

No ↓

Is the work a cycle?
i.e. A collection of independent early poems, romances, etc., in the same language, centred on a certain person, event, object, etc.

Yes → **Has the cycle a generally accepted title?**

Yes → Uniform title = the generally accepted title.
Rule 25.12A

No ↓

For a cycle identified only by a descriptive phrase enter as instructed under Rule 21.7.
Rule 25.12A

→ Go to p.20

No ↓

Then the work must be treated as an 'individual title'.

Go to p.53

Go to p.58 to establish if any additions are necessary

You have arrived here by deciding that:

An entry under TITLE is required, that a UNIFORM TITLE should be established, the work does not fall into any of the categories listed on page 36 and that the work is a COLLECTIVE TITLE (as defined on page 51).

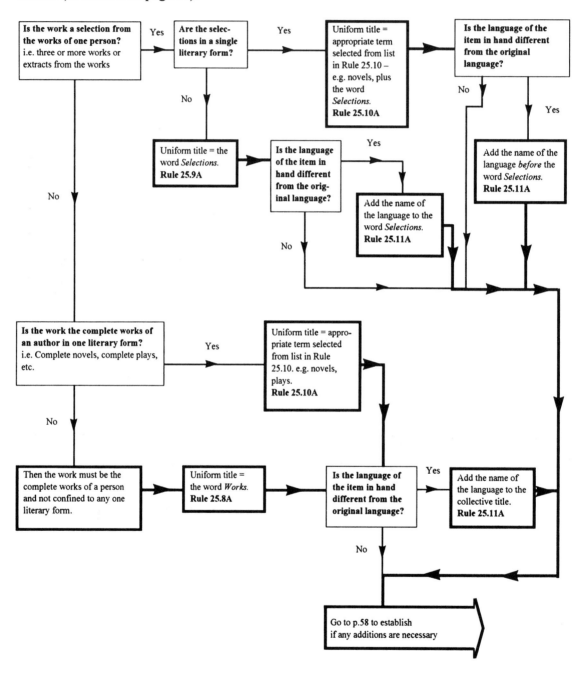

You have arrived here by deciding that:
An entry under TITLE is required, a UNIFORM TITLE should be established, that the work does not fall into any of the special categories listed on page 36 and that the work is an INDIVIDUAL TITLE.

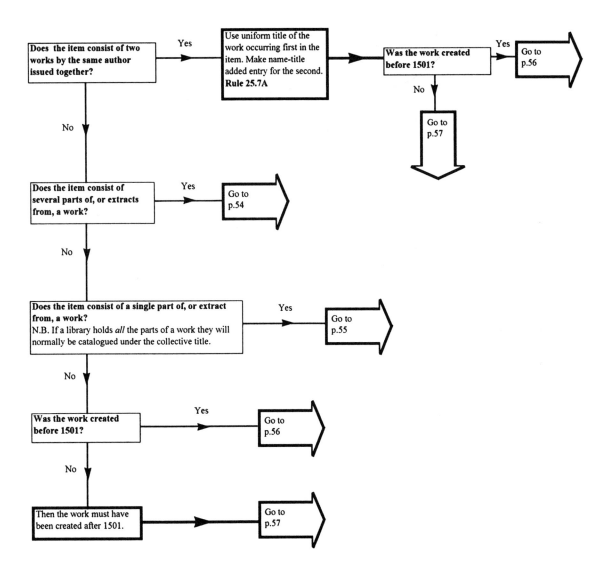

You have arrived here by deciding that:
An entry under TITLE is required, that a UNIFORM TITLE should be established, that the work does not fall into any of the special categories listed on page 54, that it is an INDIVIDUAL TITLE and that it consists of several PARTS of, or EXTRACTS from, a larger work.

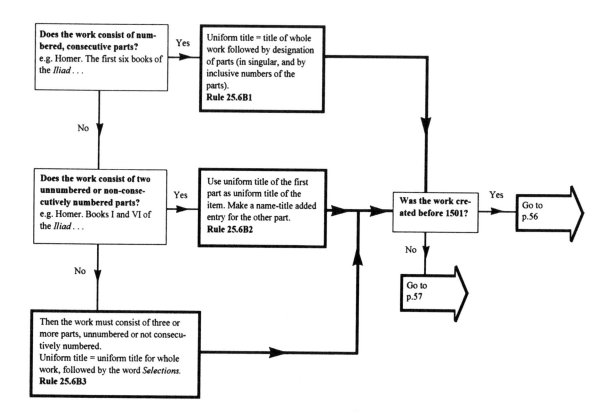

You have arrived here by deciding that:
An entry under TITLE is required, that a UNIFORM TITLE should be established, that the work does not fall into any of the special categories listed on page 36, that the item is an INDIVIDUAL TITLE and that it is a SINGLE PART of, or EXTRACT from, a work.

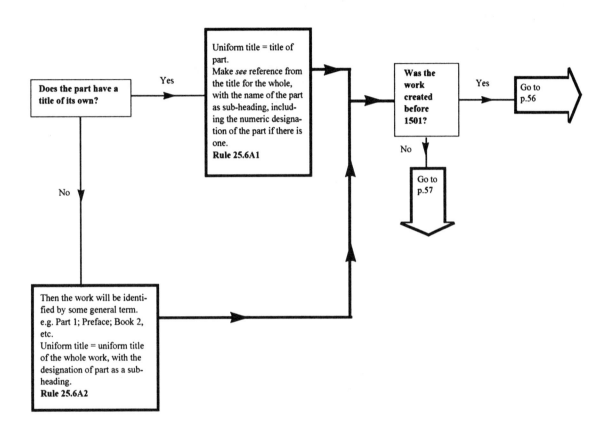

You have arrived here by deciding that:
An entry under TITLE is required, a UNIFORM TITLE should be established and that it is a SINGLE TITLE for a work created before 1501.

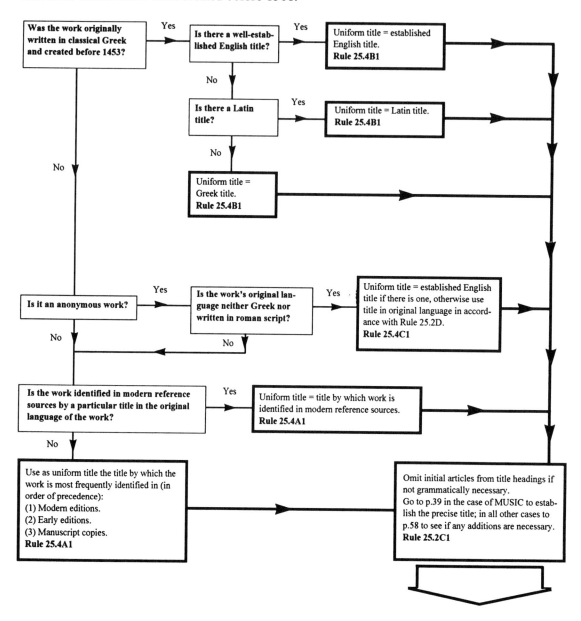

Was the work originally written in classical Greek and created before 1453? — Yes → **Is there a well-established English title?** — Yes → Uniform title = established English title. **Rule 25.4B1**

Is there a well-established English title? — No → **Is there a Latin title?** — Yes → Uniform title = Latin title. **Rule 25.4B1**

Is there a Latin title? — No → Uniform title = Greek title. **Rule 25.4B1**

Was the work originally written in classical Greek and created before 1453? — No

Is it an anonymous work? — Yes → **Is the work's original language neither Greek nor written in roman script?** — Yes → Uniform title = established English title if there is one, otherwise use title in original language in accordance with Rule 25.2D. **Rule 25.4C1**

Is it an anonymous work? — No

Is the work's original language neither Greek nor written in roman script? — No

Is the work identified in modern reference sources by a particular title in the original language of the work? — Yes → Uniform title = title by which work is identified in modern reference sources. **Rule 25.4A1**

Is the work identified in modern reference sources by a particular title in the original language of the work? — No

Use as uniform title the title by which the work is most frequently identified in (in order of precedence):
(1) Modern editions.
(2) Early editions.
(3) Manuscript copies.
Rule 25.4A1

Omit initial articles from title headings if not grammatically necessary.
Go to p.39 in the case of MUSIC to establish the precise title; in all other cases to p.58 to see if any additions are necessary.
Rule 25.2C1

You have arrived here by deciding that:
An entry under TITLE is required, a UNIFORM TITLE should be established and that it is a SINGLE TITLE for a work created after 1500.

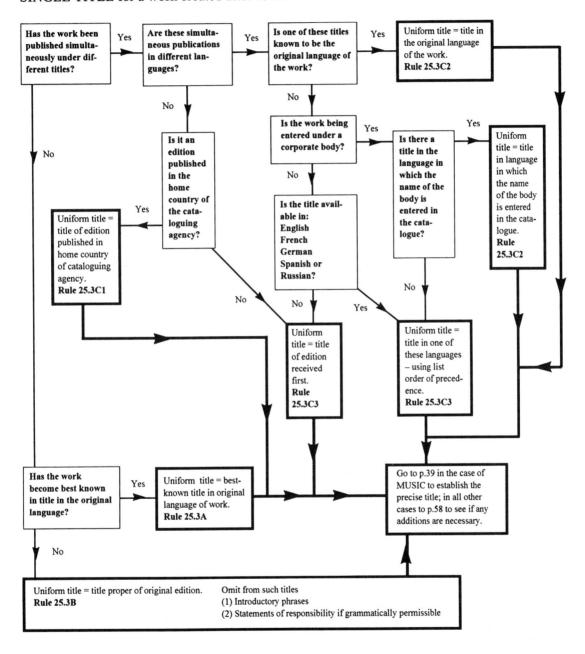

You have decided upon the UNIFORM TITLE.
Finally, it may be necessary to make some additions to this title in order to provide an absolute identification.

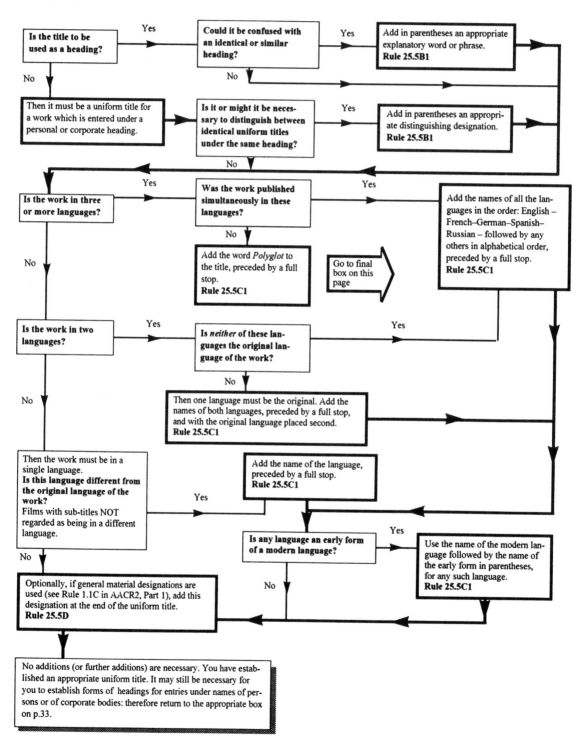

Is the title to be used as a heading? — **Yes** → Could it be confused with an identical or similar heading? — **Yes** → Add in parentheses an appropriate explanatory word or phrase. **Rule 25.5B1**

No ↓

Then it must be a uniform title for a work which is entered under a personal or corporate heading. → Is it or might it be necessary to distinguish between identical uniform titles under the same heading? — **Yes** → Add in parentheses an appropriate distinguishing designation. **Rule 25.5B1**

No ↓

Is the work in three or more languages? — **Yes** → Was the work published simultaneously in these languages? — **Yes** → Add the names of all the languages in the order: English – French–German–Spanish–Russian – followed by any others in alphabetical order, preceded by a full stop. **Rule 25.5C1**

No ↓ (Was the work published...) → **No** → Add the word *Polyglot* to the title, preceded by a full stop. **Rule 25.5C1**

Go to final box on this page

Is the work in two languages? — **Yes** → Is *neither* of these languages the original language of the work? — **Yes** →

No ↓

Then one language must be the original. Add the names of both languages, preceded by a full stop, and with the original language placed second. **Rule 25.5C1**

Then the work must be in a single language. **Is this language different from the original language of the work?** Films with sub-titles NOT regarded as being in a different language. — **Yes** → Add the name of the language, preceded by a full stop. **Rule 25.5C1**

No ↓

Is any language an early form of a modern language? — **Yes** → Use the name of the modern language followed by the name of the early form in parentheses, for any such language. **Rule 25.5C1**

No ↓

Optionally, if general material designations are used (see Rule 1.1C in AACR2, Part 1), add this designation at the end of the uniform title. **Rule 25.5D**

No additions (or further additions) are necessary. You have established an appropriate uniform title. It may still be necessary for you to establish forms of headings for entries under names of persons or of corporate bodies: therefore return to the appropriate box on p.33.

You have arrived here by deciding that:
An entry under the name of a CORPORATE BODY is required.

Note

(1) **Romanization (Rule 24.1B1)**
If the name of the body is in a language written in a non-roman script, romanize the name according to the transliteration table for that language adopted by the cataloguing agency. Refer from other romanizations as necessary.

(2) **Change of name (Rule 24.1C1)**
If the name of a corporate body has changed (including from one language to another) establish a new heading for works appearing under the new name, and connect the old and new names by references.

e.g.	Countryside Commission	National Parks Commission
	see also	*see also*
	National Parks Commission	Countryside Commission
	for earlier works of this body.	for later works of this body.

(3) If the name of a corporate body consists of or contains initials, omit or include full stops and other marks of punctuation according to the predominant usage of the body. In case of doubt, omit the full stops, etc. Do not leave a space between a full stop, etc., and an initial following it. Do not leave spaces between the letters of an initialism written without full stops, etc. (**Rule 24.1A**)

(4) **Omissions from corporate headings (Rule 24.5)**
(a) Omit an initial article unless the heading is to file under the article. (**Rule 24.5A1**)
(b) Omit phrases citing an honour awarded to the body. (**Rule 24.5B1**)
(c) Omit terms signifying the incorporation, ownership, status, etc. of organizations (e.g. Ltd., Pty., Inc.) unless they are an integral part of the name or are needed to make it clear that it is a corporate name. (**Rules 24.5C1–24.5C3**)
Omit also abbreviations such as H.M.S. and U.S.S. occurring before the name of a ship. (**Rule 24.5C4**)

(5) **References**
Make references from other forms of name for a corporate body (i.e. those not adopted as entry headings) as instructed in **Rule 26.3**.

Certain categories of corporate bodies are treated in special ways. Therefore it is first of all necessary to establish if these special provisions apply.

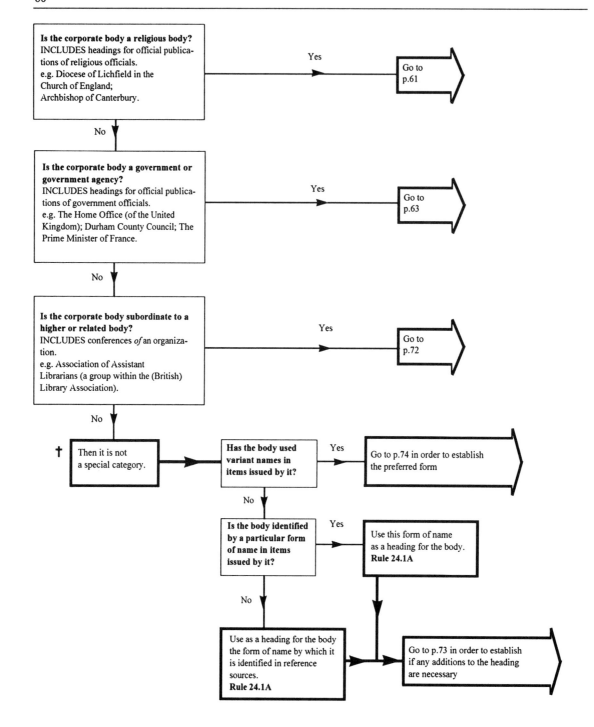

You have arrived here by deciding that:
An entry under the name of a CORPORATE BODY is required and that you are dealing with a RELIGIOUS BODY.

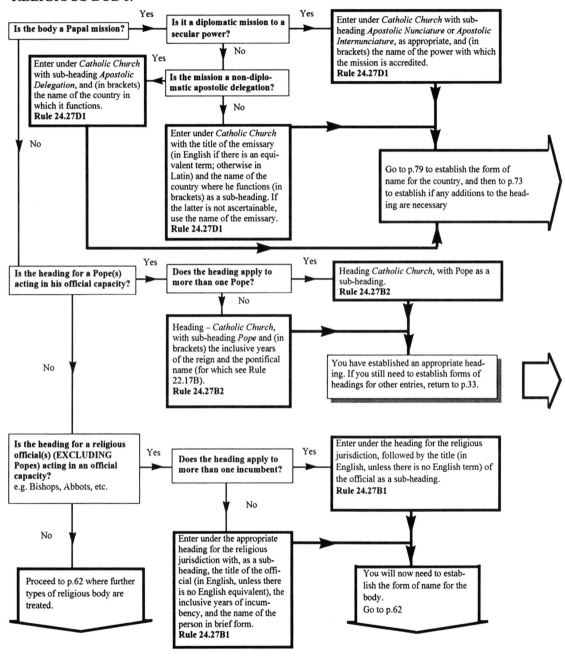

You have arrived here by deciding that:
An entry under the name of a CORPORATE BODY is required and that you are dealing with a
RELIGIOUS BODY.

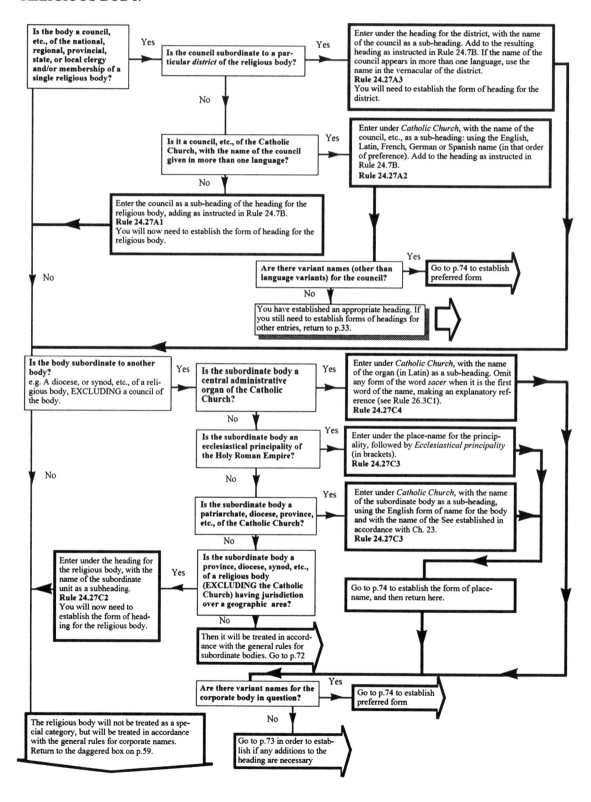

Is the body a council, etc., of the national, regional, provincial, state, or local clergy and/or membership of a single religious body?

Yes → Is the council subordinate to a particular *district* of the religious body?

Yes → Enter under the heading for the district, with the name of the council as a sub-heading. Add to the resulting heading as instructed in Rule 24.7B. If the name of the council appears in more than one language, use the name in the vernacular of the district. **Rule 24.27A3** You will need to establish the form of heading for the district.

No ↓

Is it a council, etc., of the Catholic Church, with the name of the council given in more than one language?

Yes → Enter under *Catholic Church*, with the name of the council, etc., as a sub-heading: using the English, Latin, French, German or Spanish name (in that order of preference). Add to the heading as instructed in Rule 24.7B. **Rule 24.27A2**

No ↓

Enter the council as a sub-heading of the heading for the religious body, adding as instructed in Rule 24.7B. **Rule 24.27A1** You will now need to establish the form of heading for the religious body.

Are there variant names (other than language variants) for the council?

Yes → Go to p.74 to establish preferred form

No ↓

You have established an appropriate heading. If you still need to establish forms of headings for other entries, return to p.33.

No ↓

Is the body subordinate to another body? e.g. A diocese, or synod, etc., of a religious body, EXCLUDING a council of the body.

Yes → Is the subordinate body a central administrative organ of the Catholic Church?

Yes → Enter under *Catholic Church*, with the name of the organ (in Latin) as a sub-heading. Omit any form of the word *sacer* when it is the first word of the name, making an explanatory reference (see Rule 26.3C1). **Rule 24.27C4**

No ↓

Is the subordinate body an ecclesiastical principality of the Holy Roman Empire?

Yes → Enter under the place-name for the principality, followed by *Ecclesiastical principality* (in brackets). **Rule 24.27C3**

No ↓

Is the subordinate body a patriarchate, diocese, province, etc., of the Catholic Church?

Yes → Enter under *Catholic Church*, with the name of the subordinate body as a sub-heading, using the English form of name for the body and with the name of the See established in accordance with Ch. 23. **Rule 24.27C3**

No ↓

No ↓ (left side)

Enter under the heading for the religious body, with the name of the subordinate unit as a subheading. **Rule 24.27C2** You will now need to establish the form of heading for the religious body.

Yes ← Is the subordinate body a province, diocese, synod, etc., of a religious body (EXCLUDING the Catholic Church) having jurisdiction over a geographic area?

Go to p.74 to establish the form of place-name, and then return here.

No ↓

Then it will be treated in accordance with the general rules for subordinate bodies. Go to p.72

Are there variant names for the corporate body in question?

Yes → Go to p.74 to establish preferred form

No ↓

The religious body will not be treated as a special category, but will be treated in accordance with the general rules for corporate names. Return to the daggered box on p.59.

Go to p.73 in order to establish if any additions to the heading are necessary

You have arrived here by deciding that:
An entry under the name of a CORPORATE BODY is required and that the corporate body is a GOVERNMENT or a GOVERNMENT AGENCY, or you are dealing with the heading for a GOVERNMENT OFFICIAL writing in his official capacity.

Note
Some government bodies or agencies are entered directly under their names, others are entered as sub-headings of the name of the appropriate government. The algorithms which follow will indicate which solution applies in a particular instance.
When you are directed to 'enter under the name of a government', use the 'conventional name' of the government. i.e. The geographic name, established in accordance with Chapter 23 of AACR2 (which is analysed on page 79 of this text). In exceptional cases, when the official name of the government is in common use, this is preferred. e.g. Greater London Council *not* London (England).

Some government bodies require special treatment. Choose from the types listed opposite.

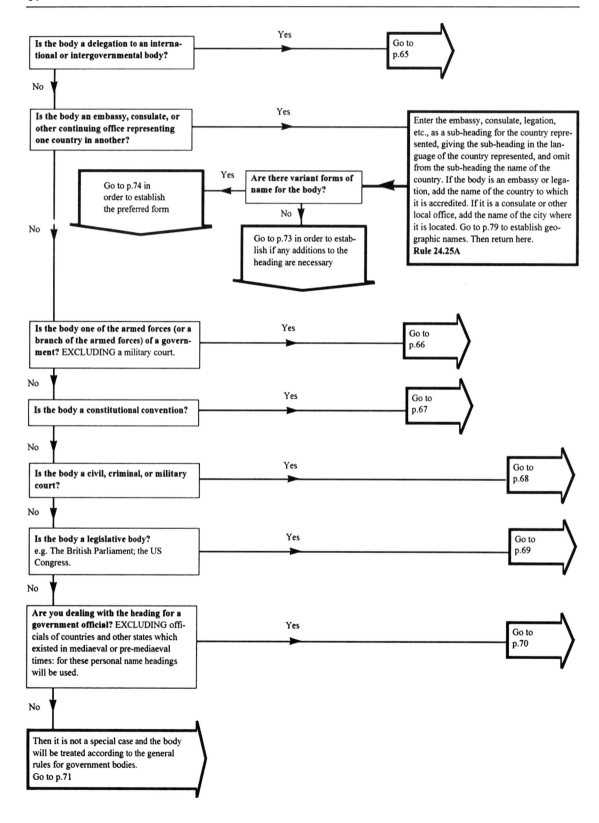

Is the body a delegation to an international or intergovernmental body?

Yes → Go to p.65

No ↓

Is the body an embassy, consulate, or other continuing office representing one country in another?

Yes → Enter the embassy, consulate, legation, etc., as a sub-heading for the country represented, giving the sub-heading in the language of the country represented, and omit from the sub-heading the name of the country. If the body is an embassy or legation, add the name of the country to which it is accredited. If it is a consulate or other local office, add the name of the city where it is located. Go to p.79 to establish geographic names. Then return here. **Rule 24.25A**

Are there variant forms of name for the body?

Yes → Go to p.74 in order to establish the preferred form

No ↓ Go to p.73 in order to establish if any additions to the heading are necessary

No ↓

Is the body one of the armed forces (or a branch of the armed forces) of a government? EXCLUDING a military court.

Yes → Go to p.66

No ↓

Is the body a constitutional convention?

Yes → Go to p.67

No ↓

Is the body a civil, criminal, or military court?

Yes → Go to p.68

No ↓

Is the body a legislative body?
e.g. The British Parliament; the US Congress.

Yes → Go to p.69

No ↓

Are you dealing with the heading for a government official? EXCLUDING officials of countries and other states which existed in mediaeval or pre-mediaeval times: for these personal name headings will be used.

Yes → Go to p.70

No ↓

Then it is not a special case and the body will be treated according to the general rules for government bodies.
Go to p.71

You have arrived here by deciding that:
An entry under the name of a CORPORATE BODY is required, the body is a GOVERNMENT AGENCY and that it is a DELEGATION TO AN INTERNATIONAL or INTERGOVERN-MENTAL BODY.

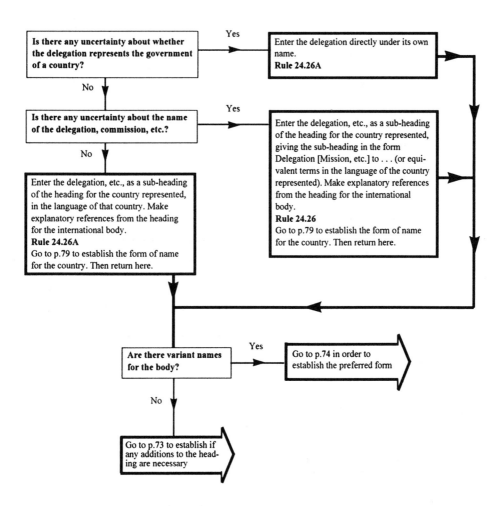

You have arrived here by deciding that:
An entry under the name of a CORPORATE BODY is required, the body is a GOVERNMENT
AGENCY and that it is one of the ARMED FORCES of a government.

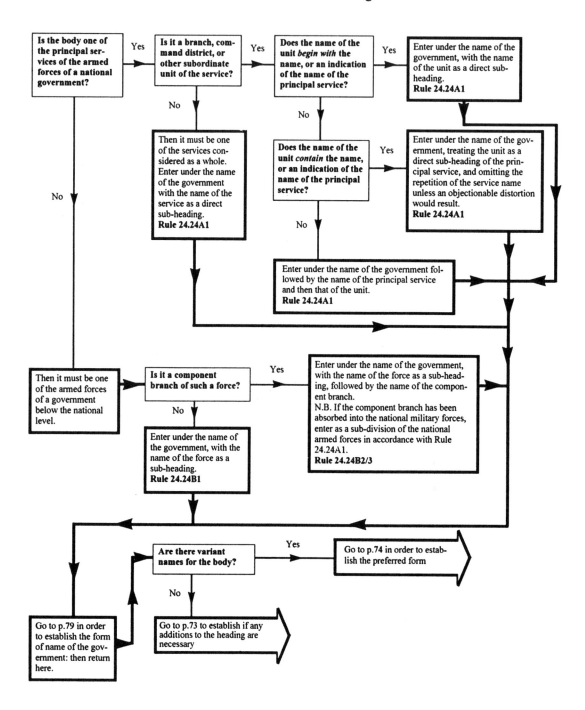

You have arrived here by deciding that:
An entry under the name of a CORPORATE BODY is required, the body is a GOVERNMENT AGENCY and that it is a CONSTITUTIONAL CONVENTION.

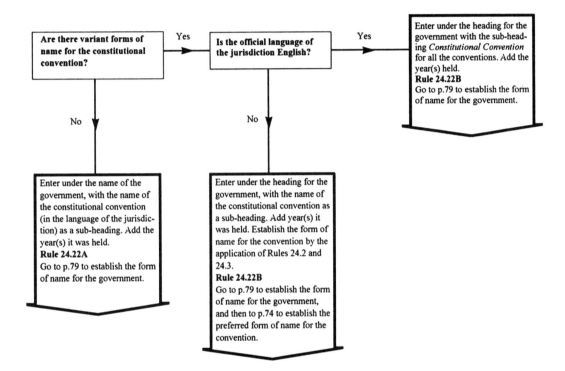

Are there variant forms of name for the constitutional convention?

Yes →

Is the official language of the jurisdiction English?

Yes →

Enter under the heading for the government with the sub-heading *Constitutional Convention* for all the conventions. Add the year(s) held.
Rule 24.22B
Go to p.79 to establish the form of name for the government.

No ↓

No ↓

Enter under the name of the government, with the name of the constitutional convention (in the language of the jurisdiction) as a sub-heading. Add the year(s) it was held.
Rule 24.22A
Go to p.79 to establish the form of name for the government.

Enter under the heading for the government, with the name of the constitutional convention as a sub-heading. Add year(s) it was held. Establish the form of name for the convention by the application of Rules 24.2 and 24.3.
Rule 24.22B
Go to p.79 to establish the form of name for the government, and then to p.74 to establish the preferred form of name for the convention.

You have arrived here by deciding that:
An entry under the name of a CORPORATE BODY is required, the body is a CORPORATE BODY and that it is a COURT OF LAW.

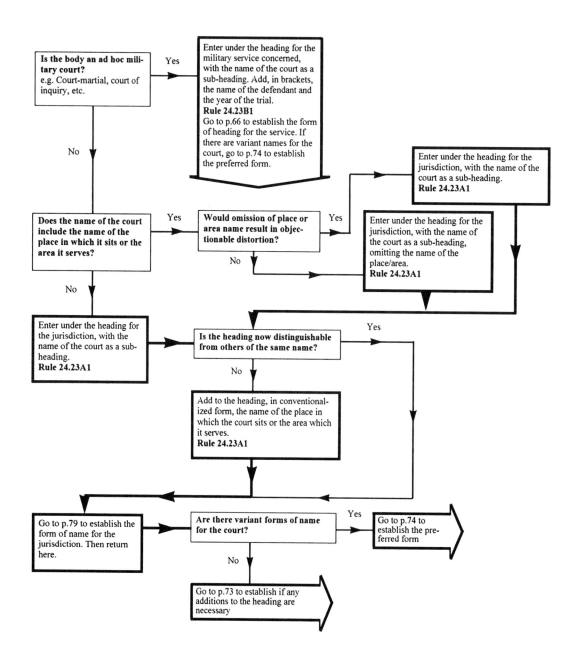

Is the body an ad hoc military court?
e.g. Court-martial, court of inquiry, etc.

Yes

Enter under the heading for the military service concerned, with the name of the court as a sub-heading. Add, in brackets, the name of the defendant and the year of the trial.
Rule 24.23B1
Go to p.66 to establish the form of heading for the service. If there are variant names for the court, go to p.74 to establish the preferred form.

No

Enter under the heading for the jurisdiction, with the name of the court as a sub-heading.
Rule 24.23A1

Does the name of the court include the name of the place in which it sits or the area it serves?

Yes

Would omission of place or area name result in objectionable distortion?

No

Yes

Enter under the heading for the jurisdiction, with the name of the court as a sub-heading, omitting the name of the place/area.
Rule 24.23A1

No

Enter under the heading for the jurisdiction, with the name of the court as a sub-heading.
Rule 24.23A1

Is the heading now distinguishable from others of the same name?

Yes

No

Add to the heading, in conventionalized form, the name of the place in which the court sits or the area which it serves.
Rule 24.23A1

Go to p.79 to establish the form of name for the jurisdiction. Then return here.

Are there variant forms of name for the court?

Yes

Go to p.74 to establish the preferred form

No

Go to p.73 to establish if any additions to the heading are necessary

You have arrived here by deciding that:
An entry under the name of a CORPORATE BODY is required, the body is a GOVERNMENT AGENCY, and it is a LEGISLATIVE BODY.

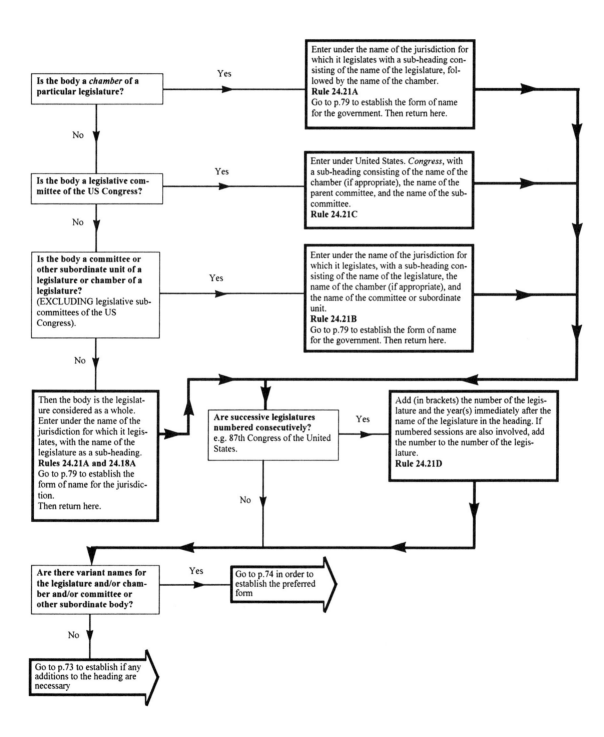

Is the body a *chamber* of a particular legislature?

Yes → Enter under the name of the jurisdiction for which it legislates with a sub-heading consisting of the name of the legislature, followed by the name of the chamber.
Rule 24.21A
Go to p.79 to establish the form of name for the government. Then return here.

No ↓

Is the body a legislative committee of the US Congress?

Yes → Enter under United States. *Congress*, with a sub-heading consisting of the name of the chamber (if appropriate), the name of the parent committee, and the name of the sub-committee.
Rule 24.21C

No ↓

Is the body a committee or other subordinate unit of a legislature or chamber of a legislature?
(EXCLUDING legislative sub-committees of the US Congress).

Yes → Enter under the name of the jurisdiction for which it legislates, with a sub-heading consisting of the name of the legislature, the name of the chamber (if appropriate), and the name of the committee or subordinate unit.
Rule 24.21B
Go to p.79 to establish the form of name for the government. Then return here.

No ↓

Then the body is the legislature considered as a whole. Enter under the name of the jurisdiction for which it legislates, with the name of the legislature as a sub-heading.
Rules 24.21A and 24.18A
Go to p.79 to establish the form of name for the jurisdiction. Then return here.

Are successive legislatures numbered consecutively?
e.g. 87th Congress of the United States.

Yes → Add (in brackets) the number of the legislature and the year(s) immediately after the name of the legislature in the heading. If numbered sessions are also involved, add the number to the number of the legislature.
Rule 24.21D

No ↓

Are there variant names for the legislature and/or chamber and/or committee or other subordinate body?

Yes → Go to p.74 in order to establish the preferred form

No ↓

Go to p.73 to establish if any additions to the heading are necessary

You have arrived here by deciding that:

An entry under the name of a CORPORATE BODY is required and that the heading is for a GOVERNMENT OFFICIAL acting in his/her official capacity.

Note

If a heading is established for the official as a person in addition to the heading for his/her official title, make an explanatory reference under the heading for the official title. See Rule 26.3C1.

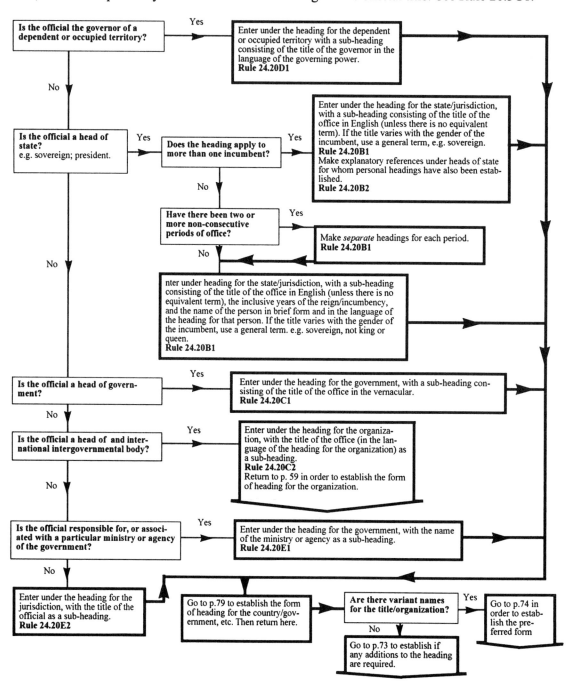

You have arrived here by deciding that:
An entry under the name of a CORPORATE BODY is required, the body is a GOVERNMENT
AGENCY and that it is NOT one of the 'special cases' identified on page 63.

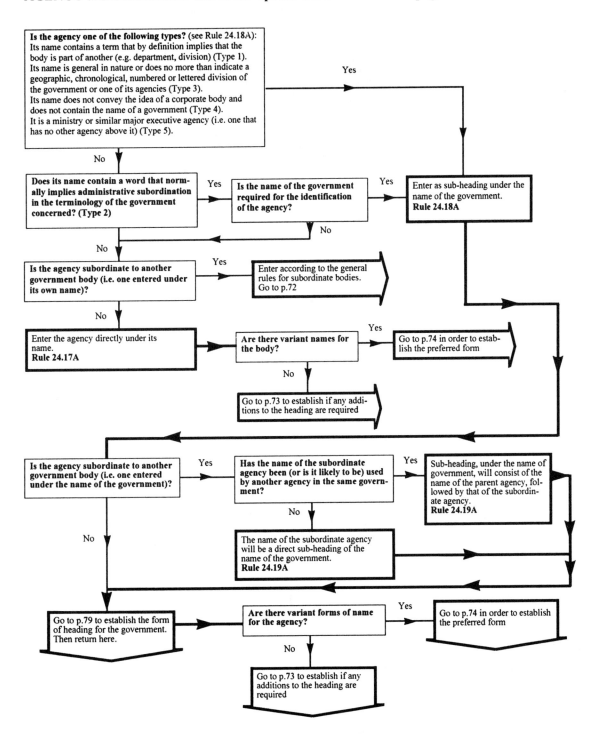

You have arrived here by deciding that:
An entry under the name of a CORPORATE BODY is required and that the body is SUBOR-DINATE or RELATED to another body.

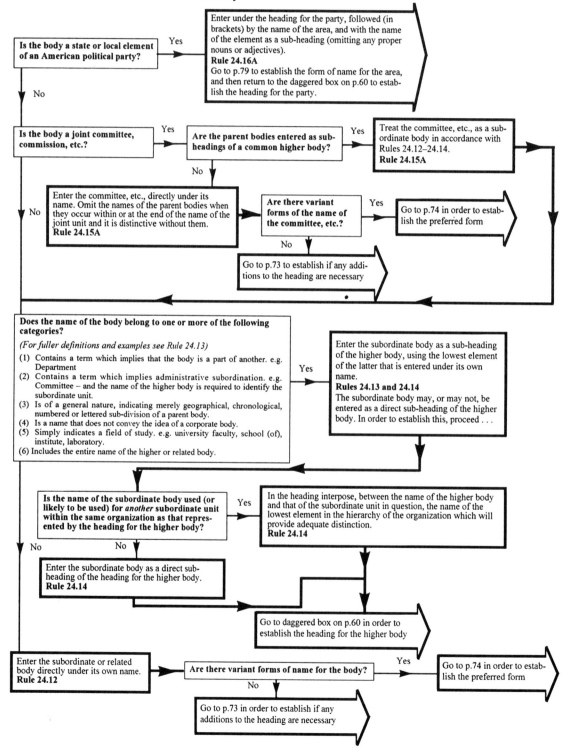

Is the body a state or local element of an American political party?

Yes → Enter under the heading for the party, followed (in brackets) by the name of the area, and with the name of the element as a sub-heading (omitting any proper nouns or adjectives).
Rule 24.16A
Go to p.79 to establish the form of name for the area, and then return to the daggered box on p.60 to establish the heading for the party.

No

Is the body a joint committee, commission, etc.?

Yes → **Are the parent bodies entered as sub-headings of a common higher body?**

Yes → Treat the committee, etc., as a subordinate body in accordance with Rules 24.12–24.14.
Rule 24.15A

No

No → Enter the committee, etc., directly under its name. Omit the names of the parent bodies when they occur within or at the end of the name of the joint unit and it is distinctive without them.
Rule 24.15A

→ **Are there variant forms of the name of the committee, etc.?**

Yes → Go to p.74 in order to establish the preferred form

No

Go to p.73 to establish if any additions to the heading are necessary

Does the name of the body belong to one or more of the following categories?

(For fuller definitions and examples see Rule 24.13)

(1) Contains a term which implies that the body is a part of another. e.g. Department
(2) Contains a term which implies administrative subordination. e.g. Committee – and the name of the higher body is required to identify the subordinate unit.
(3) Is of a general nature, indicating merely geographical, chronological, numbered or lettered sub-division of a parent body.
(4) Is a name that does not convey the idea of a corporate body.
(5) Simply indicates a field of study. e.g. university faculty, school (of), institute, laboratory.
(6) Includes the entire name of the higher or related body.

Yes → Enter the subordinate body as a sub-heading of the higher body, using the lowest element of the latter that is entered under its own name.
Rules 24.13 and 24.14
The subordinate body may, or may not, be entered as a direct sub-heading of the higher body. In order to establish this, proceed . . .

Is the name of the subordinate body used (or likely to be used) for *another* subordinate unit within the same organization as that represented by the heading for the higher body?

Yes → In the heading interpose, between the name of the higher body and that of the subordinate unit in question, the name of the lowest element in the hierarchy of the organization which will provide adequate distinction.
Rule 24.14

No   No

Enter the subordinate body as a direct sub-heading of the heading for the higher body.
Rule 24.14

Go to daggered box on p.60 in order to establish the heading for the higher body

Enter the subordinate or related body directly under its own name.
Rule 24.12

→ **Are there variant forms of name for the body?**

Yes → Go to p.74 in order to establish the preferred form

No

Go to p.73 in order to establish if any additions to the heading are necessary

You have arrived here by deciding that:

An entry under the name of a CORPORATE BODY is required. You have determined the basis of the form of heading for the body. Finally, you must establish if any further ADDITIONS to the heading are necessary.

Note

(1) All additions specified below are given in parentheses.

(2) Where the addition of a geographic name is required its form is established by the application of Chapter 23 of the Rules: treated on p.79 of the algorithm.

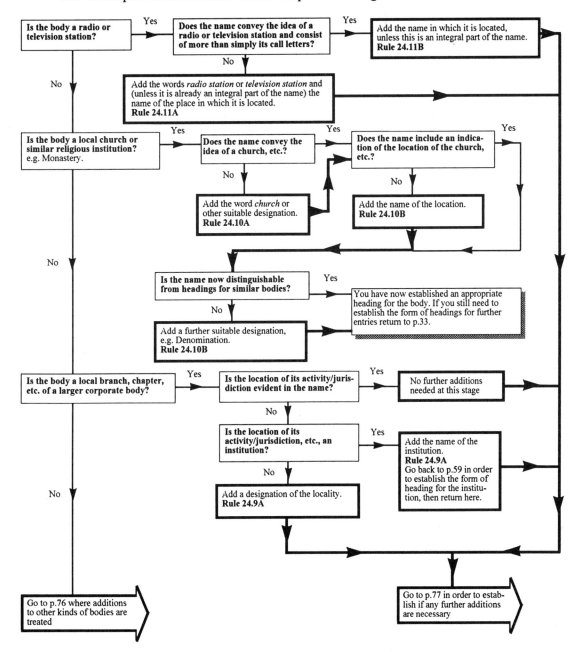

74

You have arrived here by deciding that:
An entry under the name of a CORPORATE BODY is required and that there are VARIANT FORMS of the body's name.

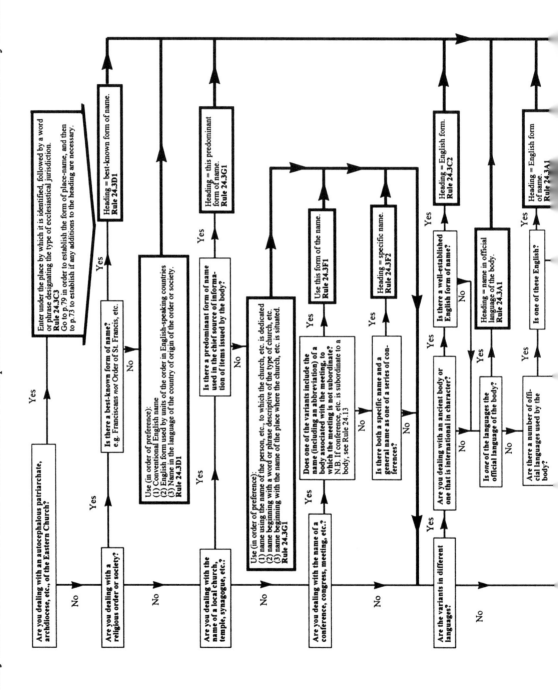

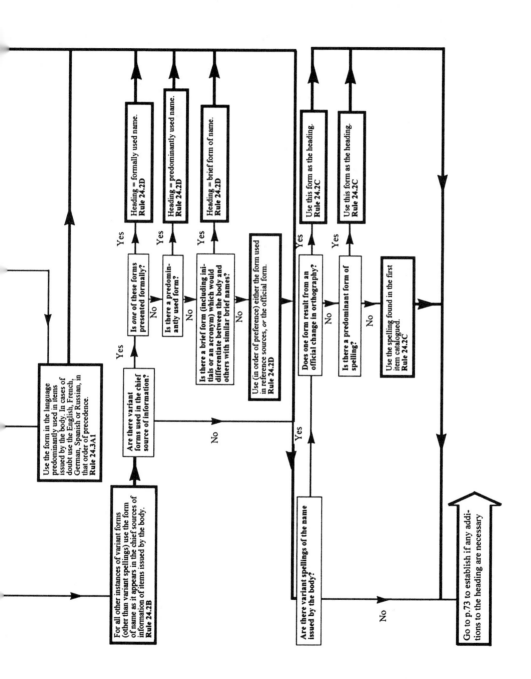

You have arrived here by deciding that:
An entry under the name of a CORPORATE BODY is required. You have determined the basis of the form of heading for the body and are now in process of checking to see if any further ADDITIONS to the heading are necessary.

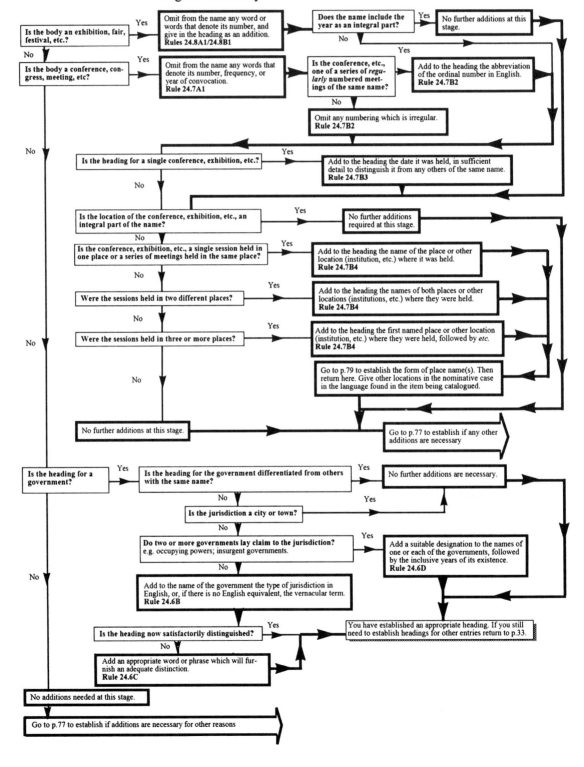

You have arrived here by deciding that:

An entry under the name of a CORPORATE BODY is required. You have determined the basis of a form of heading for the body and are now in process of checking to see if any further ADDITIONS to the heading are necessary.

Note

If the name of a local jurisdiction or geographic locality is used as an addition to the name of a body, and the name of the locality, etc. has changed during the lifetime of the body, use the latest name for the locality, etc. that has been used in the lifetime of the body. **Rule 24.4C6**

Remember

All additions specified below are given in parentheses, *and* geographic names are established in accordance with Chapter 23 of the Rules: treated on page 79 of the algorithm.

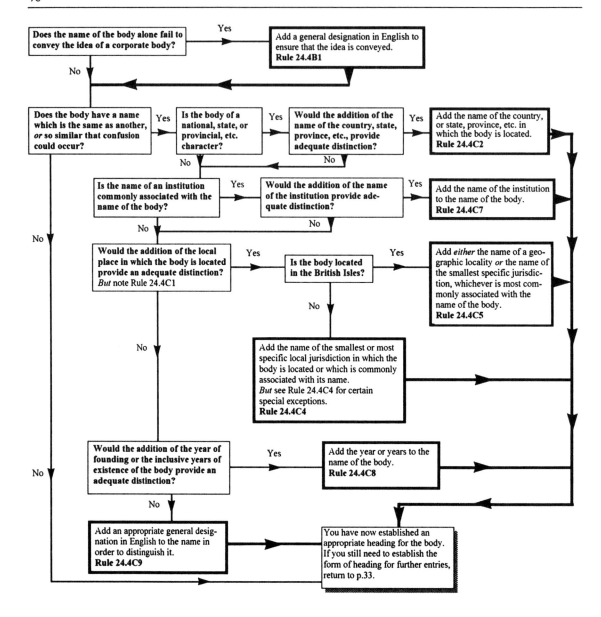

Does the name of the body alone fail to convey the idea of a corporate body?

Yes → Add a general designation in English to ensure that the idea is conveyed. **Rule 24.4B1**

No ↓

Does the body have a name which is the same as another, *or* so similar that confusion could occur?

Yes → Is the body of a national, state, or provincial, etc. character?

Yes → Would the addition of the name of the country, state, province, etc., provide adequate distinction?

Yes → Add the name of the country, or state, province, etc. in which the body is located. **Rule 24.4C2**

No ←

Is the name of an institution commonly associated with the name of the body?

Yes → Would the addition of the name of the institution provide adequate distinction?

Yes → Add the name of the institution to the name of the body. **Rule 24.4C7**

No ↓

Would the addition of the local place in which the body is located provide an adequate distinction? *But* note Rule 24.4C1

Yes → Is the body located in the British Isles?

Yes → Add *either* the name of a geographic locality *or* the name of the smallest specific jurisdiction, whichever is most commonly associated with the name of the body. **Rule 24.4C5**

No ↓

Add the name of the smallest or most specific local jurisdiction in which the body is located or which is commonly associated with its name. *But* see Rule 24.4C4 for certain special exceptions. **Rule 24.4C4**

No ↓

Would the addition of the year of founding or the inclusive years of existence of the body provide an adequate distinction?

Yes → Add the year or years to the name of the body. **Rule 24.4C8**

No ↓

Add an appropriate general designation in English to the name in order to distinguish it. **Rule 24.4C9**

→ You have now established an appropriate heading for the body. If you still need to establish the form of heading for further entries, return to p.33.

No (left column, from first question)

You have arrived here by deciding that you need to establish the form of a GEOGRAPHIC NAME to use:

(a) to distinguish between corporate bodies of the same name

or

(b) as an addition to other corporate names

or

(c) as a heading for a government.

Note

(1) *Changes of name.* If the name of a place changes (whether the name of a government or the name of a place being added to a heading) use the name appropriate in time for the heading under consideration. **See Rule 23.3A**. This decision having been made, the *form* of the name will then be determined by using the algorithm which follows.

(2) *Form of name for the United Kingdom.* The rules in Chapter 23, and examples elsewhere in AACR2, imply the use of the form 'United Kingdom' for the geo-political entity of the 'United Kingdom of Great Britain and Northern Ireland'. However, the form traditionally used in catalogues, etc., for this jurisdiction is 'Great Britain'. Both the British Library and the Library of Congress have indicated their intentions to retain 'Great Britain' in their cataloguing procedures – and the solutions to the examples accompanying this text conform to this decision, i.e. they use the form 'Great Britain'.

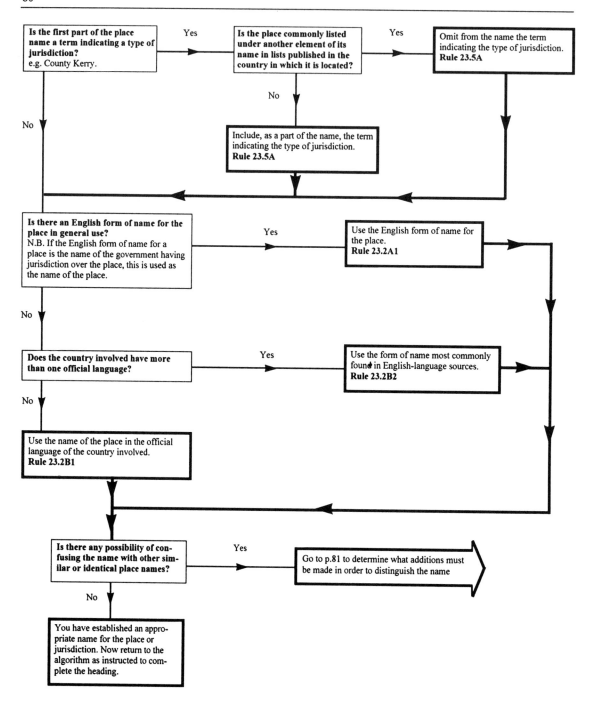

Is the first part of the place name a term indicating a type of jurisdiction?
e.g. County Kerry.

Yes →

Is the place commonly listed under another element of its name in lists published in the country in which it is located?

Yes →

Omit from the name the term indicating the type of jurisdiction.
Rule 23.5A

No ↓

Include, as a part of the name, the term indicating the type of jurisdiction.
Rule 23.5A

No ↓

Is there an English form of name for the place in general use?
N.B. If the English form of name for a place is the name of the government having jurisdiction over the place, this is used as the name of the place.

Yes →

Use the English form of name for the place.
Rule 23.2A1

No ↓

Does the country involved have more than one official language?

Yes →

Use the form of name most commonly found in English-language sources.
Rule 23.2B2

No ↓

Use the name of the place in the official language of the country involved.
Rule 23.2B1

Is there any possibility of confusing the name with other similar or identical place names?

Yes →

Go to p.81 to determine what additions must be made in order to distinguish the name

No ↓

You have established an appropriate name for the place or jurisdiction. Now return to the algorithm as instructed to complete the heading.

You have arrived here by deciding that you need to make some ADDITIONS to a GEOGRAPH-ICAL NAME in order to distinguish between identical or similar names for places or jurisdictions.

Note

(1) All additions to place names as entry elements are given in parentheses. e.g. Budapest (Hungary). **Rule 23.4A1**

(2) If the place name is being used as an addition, precede the name of the larger place by a comma. e.g. St Peter's Church (York, England). **Rule 23.4A1**

(3) Place names used as additions may be abbreviated in accordance with the instructions in Appendix B.14 of the Rules. **Rule 23.4B1**

(4) Note certain options concerning additions detailed in **Rule 23.4B1.**

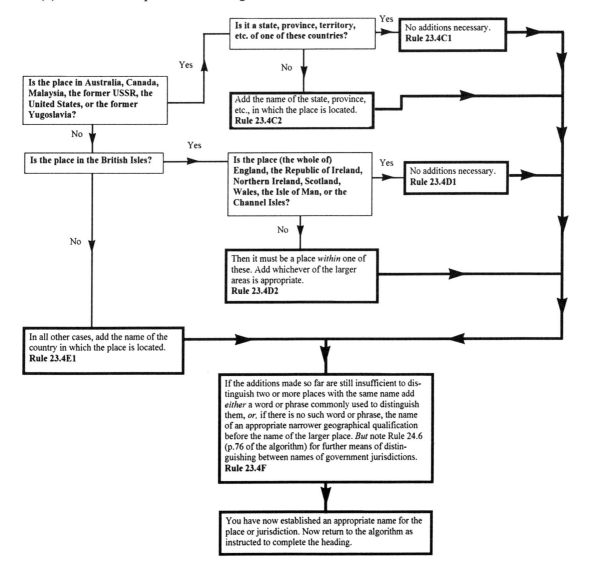

You have arrived here by deciding that:
An entry under the name of a PERSON is required.

Note

(1) The basis of the heading for a person is the name by which he or she is commonly identified. This may be the person's real name, pseudonym, title of nobility, initials, nickname or other appellation. Treat a roman numeral associated with a given name as part of the name. **Rule 22.1A**

(2) Establish the name by which a person is commonly identified from the *chief source of information* (see Rule 1.0A in Part I of the Rules) of the works of that person issued in his or her language. If the person works in a non-verbal context (e.g. a painter, a sculptor) or is not known primarily as an author, determine the name by which he or she is commonly known from reference sources issued in his or her language or country of residence or activity. **Rule 22.1B**

(3) Accents and other diacritical marks are included in the name, and are supplied if they are an integral part of the name but have been omitted in the source from which the name is taken. **Rule 22.1D1**

(4) Hyphens are retained in the name if they are used by the bearer of the name or if they are prescribed by the romanization system adapted by the cataloguing agency. However, hyphens which join a person's forename(s) to the surname are omitted. **Rule 22.1D2**

A person may be known by *different names* (e.g. the real name and a pseudonym), or by *different forms of the same name* (e.g. Joan of Arc *and* Jeanne d'Arc). If so, you must first decide which of the names (or different forms of the name) you should prefer as the heading for that person.

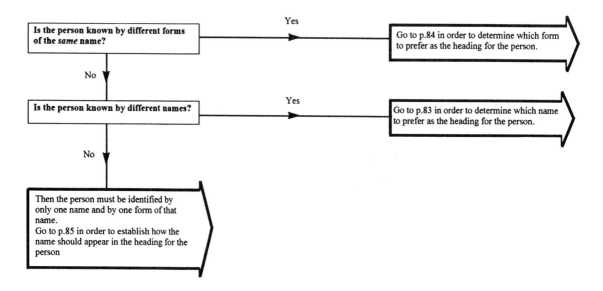

You have arrived here by deciding that:
An entry under the name of a PERSON is required and that the person is or has been known by DIFFERENT NAMES. Before proceeding further consult **Rule 22.2B2** of the code to establish what is meant by the concept of SEPARATE BIBLIOGRAPHIC IDENTITIES. In all cases make references as specified under **Rules 26.2B, 26.2C, 26.2D.**

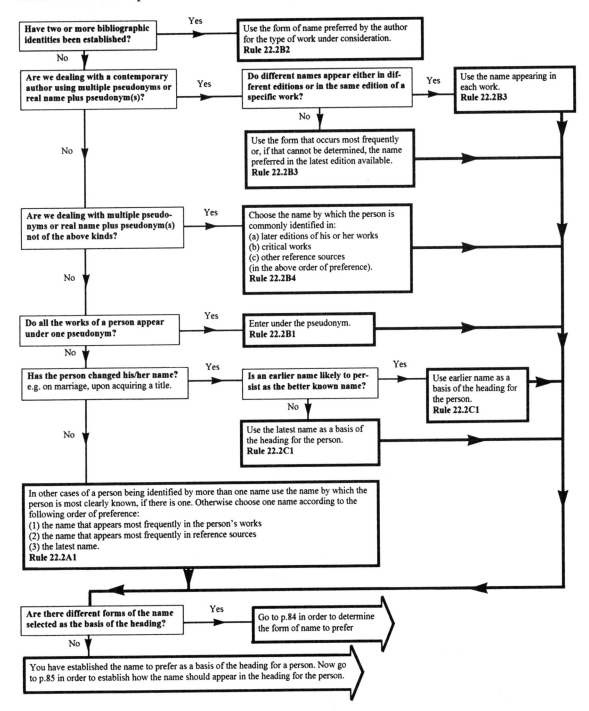

You have arrived here by deciding that:
An entry under the name of a PERSON is required and that the person is or has been known by
DIFFERENT FORMS of the same name.

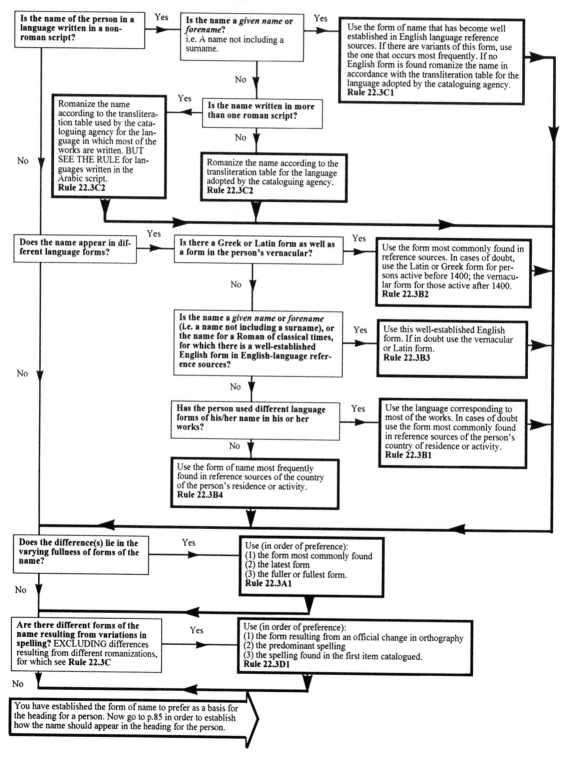

Is the name of the person in a language written in a non-roman script?	Yes → **Is the name a *given name* or *forename*?** i.e. A name not including a surname. → Yes → Use the form of name that has become well established in English language reference sources. If there are variants of this form, use the one that occurs most frequently. If no English form is found romanize the name in accordance with the transliteration table for the language adopted by the cataloguing agency. **Rule 22.3C1**

Romanize the name according to the translitera-tion table used by the cata-loguing agency for the lan-guage in which most of the works are written. BUT SEE THE RULE for lan-guages written in the Arabic script. **Rule 22.3C2**

Yes ← **Is the name written in more than one roman script?**

No ↓

Romanize the name according to the transliteration table for the language adopted by the cataloguing agency. **Rule 22.3C2**

Does the name appear in dif-ferent language forms? — Yes → **Is there a Greek or Latin form as well as a form in the person's vernacular?** — Yes → Use the form most commonly found in reference sources. In cases of doubt, use the Latin or Greek form for per-sons active before 1400; the vernacu-lar form for those active after 1400. **Rule 22.3B2**

No ↓

Is the name a *given name* or *forename* (i.e. a name not including a surname), or the name for a Roman of classical times, for which there is a well-established English form in English-language refer-ence sources? — Yes → Use this well-established English form. If in doubt use the vernacular or Latin form. **Rule 22.3B3**

No ↓

Has the person used different language forms of his/her name in his or her works? — Yes → Use the language corresponding to most of the works. In cases of doubt use the form most commonly found in reference sources of the person's country of residence or activity. **Rule 22.3B1**

No ↓

Use the form of name most frequently found in reference sources of the country of the person's residence or activity. **Rule 22.3B4**

Does the difference(s) lie in the varying fullness of forms of the name? — Yes → Use (in order of preference): (1) the form most commonly found (2) the latest form (3) the fuller or fullest form. **Rule 22.3A1**

No ↓

Are there different forms of the name resulting from variations in spelling? EXCLUDING differences resulting from different romanizations, for which see **Rule 22.3C** — Yes → Use (in order of preference): (1) the form resulting from an official change in orthography (2) the predominant spelling (3) the spelling found in the first item catalogued. **Rule 22.3D1**

No ↓

You have established the form of name to prefer as a basis for the heading for a person. Now go to p.85 in order to establish how the name should appear in the heading for the person.

You have arrived here by deciding that:

An entry under the name of a PERSON is required. You have chosen the basis for the heading, and now need to establish the way in which the name will appear in the heading. The form and usage of names in non-Western cultures may be unfamiliar. Therefore, special rules are provided for names in certain foreign languages: these indicate the entry element for such names, and their structure in a heading.

Note

(1) Whilst these special rules will generally be self-sufficient in handling names in the languages to which they relate, occasionally it may be necessary to refer to the general rules in Chapter 22 (or to the appropriate point in the algorithm dealing with this chapter).

(2) In particular, Rules 22.18–22.19 (page 96 of the algorithm) will apply if it is necessary to distinguish between identical names.

(3) Much more comprehensive and detailed guidance on the handling of personal names is given in – *Names of persons: national usages for entry in catalogues*, compiled by the IFLA Office for UBC, 3rd edn, London, The Office, 1977.

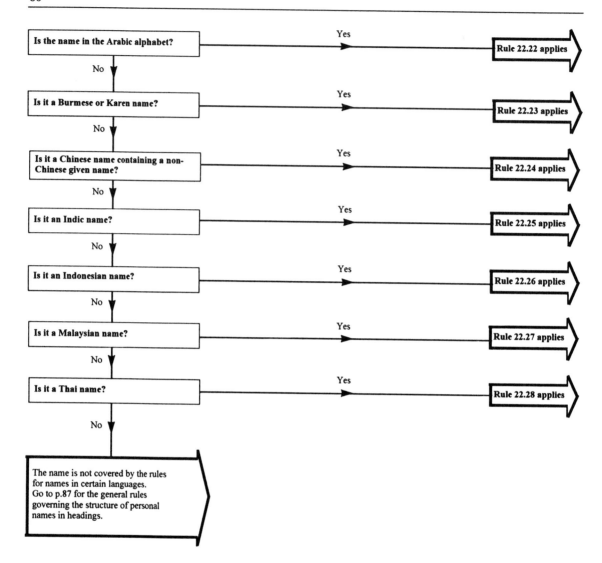

Is the name in the Arabic alphabet? — Yes → Rule 22.22 applies

No ↓

Is it a Burmese or Karen name? — Yes → Rule 22.23 applies

No ↓

Is it a Chinese name containing a non-Chinese given name? — Yes → Rule 22.24 applies

No ↓

Is it an Indic name? — Yes → Rule 22.25 applies

No ↓

Is it an Indonesian name? — Yes → Rule 22.26 applies

No ↓

Is it a Malaysian name? — Yes → Rule 22.27 applies

No ↓

Is it a Thai name? — Yes → Rule 22.28 applies

No ↓

The name is not covered by the rules for names in certain languages.
Go to p.87 for the general rules governing the structure of personal names in headings.

You have arrived here by deciding that:
An entry under the name of a PERSON is required. You have selected the name to be used as the basis of the heading for the person. You now need to determine HOW the name should appear in the heading: notably, to establish what the *entry element* will be. In addition, you have decided that the name is not covered by the special rules for names in certain languages which are listed on page 85 of this algorithm.

Note

(1) If a person's name consists of several parts, select as entry element that part of the name under which the person would normally be listed in authoritative alphabetic lists in his or her language or country of residence or activity. **Rule 22.4A**

(2) Rules 22.5–22.9 (to which the next section of the algorithm relates) conform to and support this general ruling. If, however, a person's known preference conflicts with the Rules, follow that preference. **Rule 22.4A**

(3) If the entry element is the first element of the name, enter the name in direct order. e.g. Ram Gopal. **Rule 22.4B1**

(4) If the first element is a surname, follow it by a comma. e.g. Name – Foo Kwac Wah: Foo being the surname. Heading takes the form – Foo, Kwac Wah. **Rule 22.4B2**

(5) If the entry element is not the first element of the name, transpose the elements of the name preceding the entry element. Follow the entry element by a comma. e.g. Name – John Doe. Heading takes the form – Doe, John. **Rule 22.4B3**

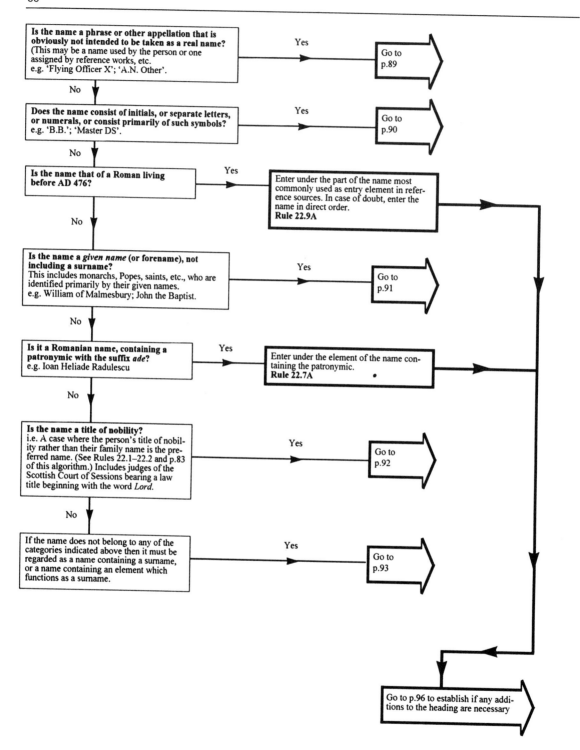

Is the name a phrase or other appellation that is obviously not intended to be taken as a real name? (This may be a name used by the person or one assigned by reference works, etc. e.g. 'Flying Officer X'; 'A.N. Other'.

Yes → Go to p.89

No ↓

Does the name consist of initials, or separate letters, or numerals, or consist primarily of such symbols? e.g. 'B.B.'; 'Master DS'.

Yes → Go to p.90

No ↓

Is the name that of a Roman living before AD 476?

Yes → Enter under the part of the name most commonly used as entry element in reference sources. In case of doubt, enter the name in direct order. **Rule 22.9A**

No ↓

Is the name a *given name* (or forename), not including a surname? This includes monarchs, Popes, saints, etc., who are identified primarily by their given names. e.g. William of Malmesbury; John the Baptist.

Yes → Go to p.91

No ↓

Is it a Romanian name, containing a patronymic with the suffix *ade*? e.g. Ioan Heliade Radulescu

Yes → Enter under the element of the name containing the patronymic. **Rule 22.7A**

No ↓

Is the name a title of nobility? i.e. A case where the person's title of nobility rather than their family name is the preferred name. (See Rules 22.1–22.2 and p.83 of this algorithm.) Includes judges of the Scottish Court of Sessions bearing a law title beginning with the word *Lord*.

Yes → Go to p.92

No ↓

If the name does not belong to any of the categories indicated above then it must be regarded as a name containing a surname, or a name containing an element which functions as a surname.

Yes → Go to p.93

Go to p.96 to establish if any additions to the heading are necessary

You have arrived here by deciding that:
An entry under the name of a PERSON is required and that the name consists of a PHRASE (or other appellation obviously not intended to be taken as a real name).

Note
Where such a phrase, etc., is used as a heading and it does not convey the idea of a person, add a suitable designation in English. e.g. River (Writer); Taj Mahal (Musician).

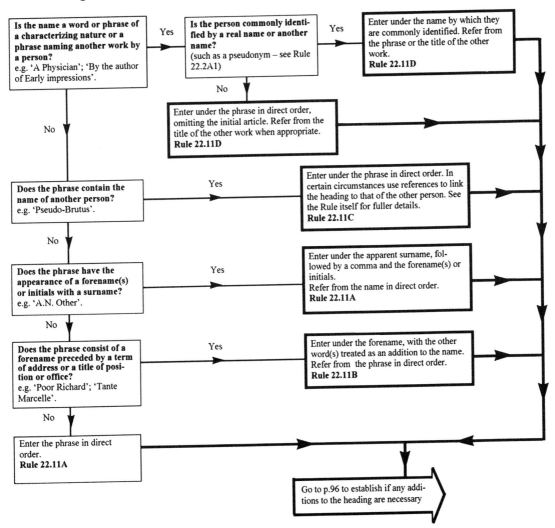

Is the name a word or phrase of a characterizing nature or a phrase naming another work by a person?
e.g. 'A Physician'; 'By the author of Early impressions'.

Yes → Is the person commonly identified by a real name or another name?
(such as a pseudonym – see Rule 22.2A1)

Yes → Enter under the name by which they are commonly identified. Refer from the phrase or the title of the other work.
Rule 22.11D

No → Enter under the phrase in direct order, omitting the initial article. Refer from title of the other work when appropriate.
Rule 22.11D

No ↓

Does the phrase contain the name of another person?
e.g. 'Pseudo-Brutus'.

Yes → Enter under the phrase in direct order. In certain circumstances use references to link the heading to that of the other person. See the Rule itself for fuller details.
Rule 22.11C

No ↓

Does the phrase have the appearance of a forename(s) or initials with a surname?
e.g. 'A.N. Other'.

Yes → Enter under the apparent surname, followed by a comma and the forename(s) or initials.
Refer from the name in direct order.
Rule 22.11A

No ↓

Does the phrase consist of a forename preceded by a term of address or a title of position or office?
e.g. 'Poor Richard'; 'Tante Marcelle'.

Yes → Enter under the forename, with the other word(s) treated as an addition to the name. Refer from the phrase in direct order.
Rule 22.11B

No ↓

Enter the phrase in direct order.
Rule 22.11A

Go to p.96 to establish if any additions to the heading are necessary

You have arrived here by deciding that:

An entry under the name of a PERSON is required and that the name consists of INITIALS, or SEPARATE LETTERS, or NUMERALS, or consists primarily of such symbols.

Note

Identifications consisting of predominantly non-alphabetic or non-numeric devices (e.g. @@??@@; or M@@@) are not regarded as names. Works whose authorship is indicated only in this way are entered under title. *See* **Rule 21.5C.**

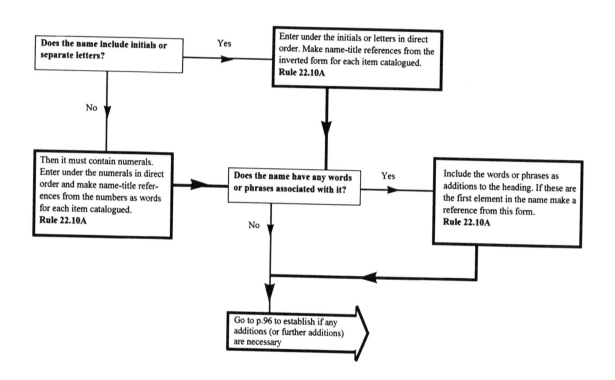

You have arrived here by deciding that:
An entry under the name of a PERSON is required and that the name is a GIVEN name. Remember that a roman numeral associated with a given name is treated as part of the name (see page 82).

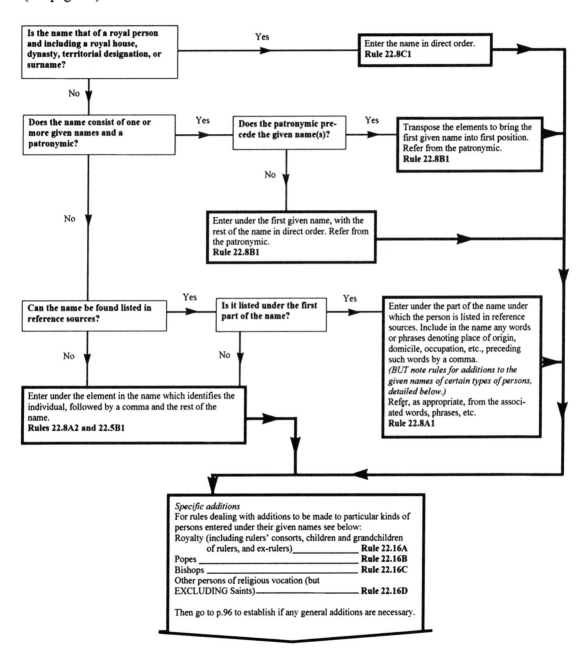

Is the name that of a royal person and including a royal house, dynasty, territorial designation, or surname?

Yes → Enter the name in direct order. **Rule 22.8C1**

No ↓

Does the name consist of one or more given names and a patronymic?

Yes → Does the patronymic precede the given name(s)?

Yes → Transpose the elements to bring the first given name into first position. Refer from the patronymic. **Rule 22.8B1**

No ↓

Enter under the first given name, with the rest of the name in direct order. Refer from the patronymic. **Rule 22.8B1**

No ↓

Can the name be found listed in reference sources?

Yes → Is it listed under the first part of the name?

Yes → Enter under the part of the name under which the person is listed in reference sources. Include in the name any words or phrases denoting place of origin, domicile, occupation, etc., preceding such words by a comma.
(BUT note rules for additions to the given names of certain types of persons, detailed below.)
Refer, as appropriate, from the associated words, phrases, etc.
Rule 22.8A1

No ↓

No ↓

Enter under the element in the name which identifies the individual, followed by a comma and the rest of the name. **Rules 22.8A2 and 22.5B1**

Specific additions
For rules dealing with additions to be made to particular kinds of persons entered under their given names see below:
Royalty (including rulers' consorts, children and grandchildren of rulers, and ex-rulers)_____ **Rule 22.16A**
Popes _____ **Rule 22.16B**
Bishops _____ **Rule 22.16C**
Other persons of religious vocation (but EXCLUDING Saints)_____ **Rule 22.16D**

Then go to p.96 to establish if any general additions are necessary.

You have arrived here by deciding that:

An entry under the name of a PERSON is required and that the name is a title of nobility (including judges of the Scottish Court of Sessions bearing a law title beginning with the word *Lord*).

Note

This section of the algorithm applies only to cases where the title (rather than the family name) has been established as the preferred name for the person. See Rules 22.1–22.2 and page 83 of the algorithm.

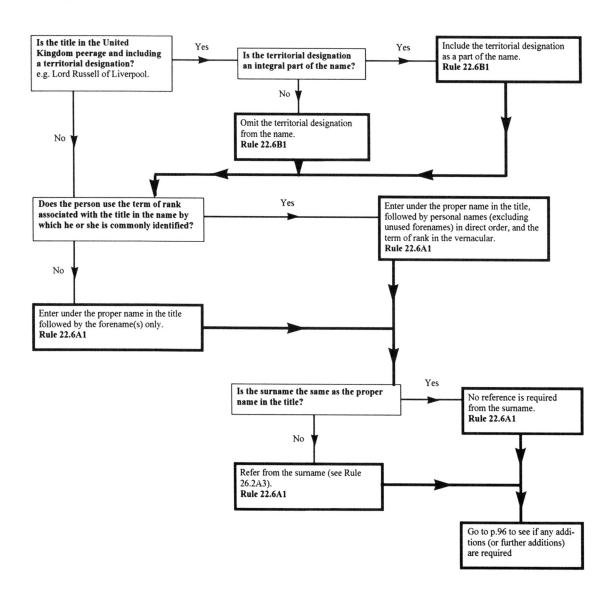

You have arrived here by deciding that:
An entry under the name of a PERSON is required and that the name contains a SURNAME or
an element FUNCTIONING AS A SURNAME.

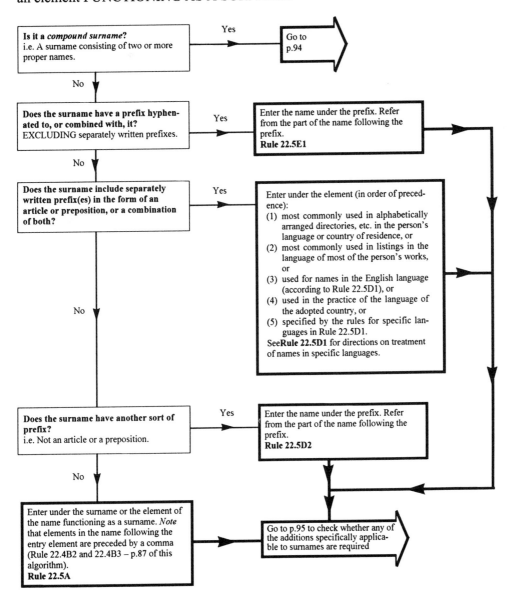

Is it a *compound surname*?
i.e. A surname consisting of two or more
proper names.

Yes → Go to
p.94

No ↓

**Does the surname have a prefix hyphen-
ated to, or combined with, it?**
EXCLUDING separately written prefixes.

Yes → Enter the name under the prefix. Refer
from the part of the name following the
prefix.
Rule 22.5E1

No ↓

**Does the surname include separately
written prefix(es) in the form of an
article or preposition, or a combination
of both?**

Yes → Enter under the element (in order of precedence):
(1) most commonly used in alphabetically
arranged directories, etc. in the person's
language or country of residence, or
(2) most commonly used in listings in the
language of most of the person's works,
or
(3) used for names in the English language
(according to Rule 22.5D1), or
(4) used in the practice of the language of
the adopted country, or
(5) specified by the rules for specific languages in Rule 22.5D1.
See **Rule 22.5D1** for directions on treatment
of names in specific languages.

No ↓

**Does the surname have another sort of
prefix?**
i.e. Not an article or a preposition.

Yes → Enter the name under the prefix. Refer
from the part of the name following the
prefix.
Rule 22.5D2

No ↓

Enter under the surname or the element of
the name functioning as a surname. *Note*
that elements in the name following the
entry element are preceded by a comma
(Rule 22.4B2 and 22.4B3 – p.87 of this
algorithm).
Rule 22.5A

→ Go to p.95 to check whether any of
the additions specifically applicable to surnames are required

You have arrived here by deciding that:
An entry under the name of a PERSON is required and that you are dealing with a COMPOUND SURNAME.

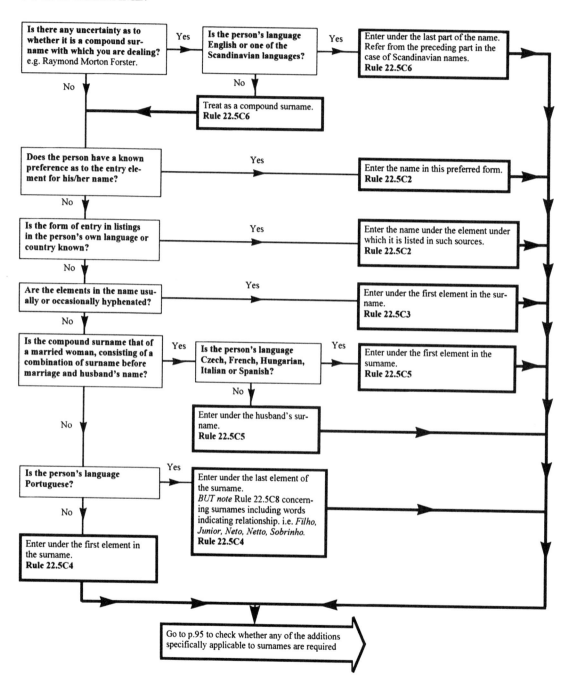

Is there any uncertainty as to whether it is a compound surname with which you are dealing? e.g. Raymond Morton Forster.

Yes → Is the person's language English or one of the Scandinavian languages?

Yes → Enter under the last part of the name. Refer from the preceding part in the case of Scandinavian names. **Rule 22.5C6**

No → Treat as a compound surname. **Rule 22.5C6**

No ↓

Does the person have a known preference as to the entry element for his/her name?

Yes → Enter the name in this preferred form. **Rule 22.5C2**

No ↓

Is the form of entry in listings in the person's own language or country known?

Yes → Enter the name under the element under which it is listed in such sources. **Rule 22.5C2**

No ↓

Are the elements in the name usually or occasionally hyphenated?

Yes → Enter under the first element in the surname. **Rule 22.5C3**

No ↓

Is the compound surname that of a married woman, consisting of a combination of surname before marriage and husband's name?

Yes → Is the person's language Czech, French, Hungarian, Italian or Spanish?

Yes → Enter under the first element in the surname. **Rule 22.5C5**

No → Enter under the husband's surname. **Rule 22.5C5**

No ↓

Is the person's language Portuguese?

Yes → Enter under the last element of the surname. *BUT note* Rule 22.5C8 concerning surnames including words indicating relationship. i.e. *Filho, Junior, Neto, Netto, Sobrinho.* **Rule 22.5C4**

No ↓

Enter under the first element in the surname. **Rule 22.5C4**

Go to p.95 to check whether any of the additions specifically applicable to surnames are required

You have arrived here to decide about ADDITIONS which may be required specifically for the headings of PERSONS entered under their SURNAME.

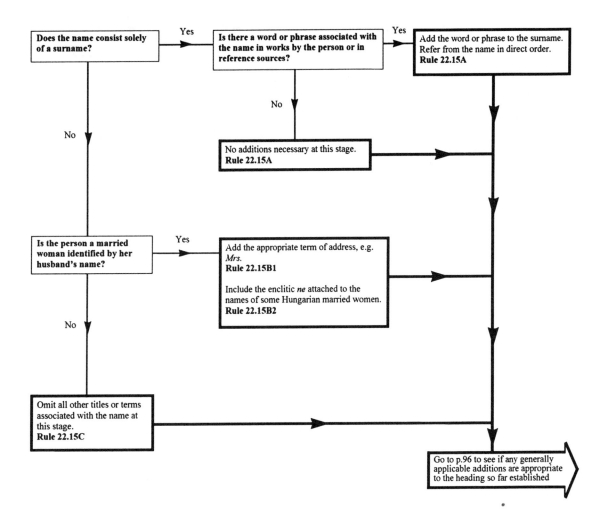

You have arrived here to decide about ADDITIONS which may be generally applicable to headings for PERSONS.

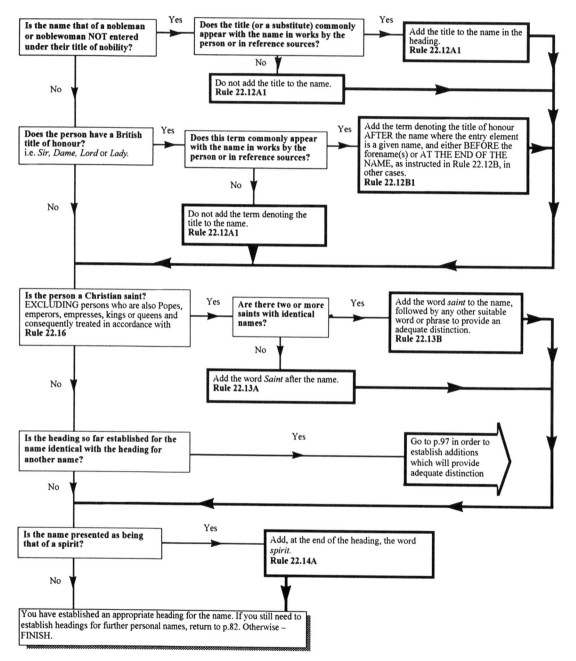

Is the name that of a nobleman or noblewoman NOT entered under their title of nobility? — Yes → **Does the title (or a substitute) commonly appear with the name in works by the person or in reference sources?** — Yes → Add the title to the name in the heading. **Rule 22.12A1**

No → Do not add the title to the name. **Rule 22.12A1**

No ↓

Does the person have a British title of honour? i.e. *Sir, Dame, Lord* or *Lady.* — Yes → **Does this term commonly appear with the name in works by the person or in reference sources?** — Yes → Add the term denoting the title of honour AFTER the name where the entry element is a given name, and either BEFORE the forename(s) or AT THE END OF THE NAME, as instructed in Rule 22.12B, in other cases. **Rule 22.12B1**

No → Do not add the term denoting the title to the name. **Rule 22.12A1**

No ↓

Is the person a Christian saint? EXCLUDING persons who are also Popes, emperors, empresses, kings or queens and consequently treated in accordance with **Rule 22.16** — Yes → **Are there two or more saints with identical names?** — Yes → Add the word *saint* to the name, followed by any other suitable word or phrase to provide an adequate distinction. **Rule 22.13B**

No → Add the word *Saint* after the name. **Rule 22.13A**

No ↓

Is the heading so far established for the name identical with the heading for another name? — Yes → Go to p.97 in order to establish additions which will provide adequate distinction

No ↓

Is the name presented as being that of a spirit? — Yes → Add, at the end of the heading, the word *spirit*. **Rule 22.14A**

No ↓

You have established an appropriate heading for the name. If you still need to establish headings for further personal names, return to p.82. Otherwise – FINISH.

You have arrived here to decide the ADDITIONS which you should make in order to distinguish the heading for the name of a PERSON which is IDENTICAL with the heading for another person.

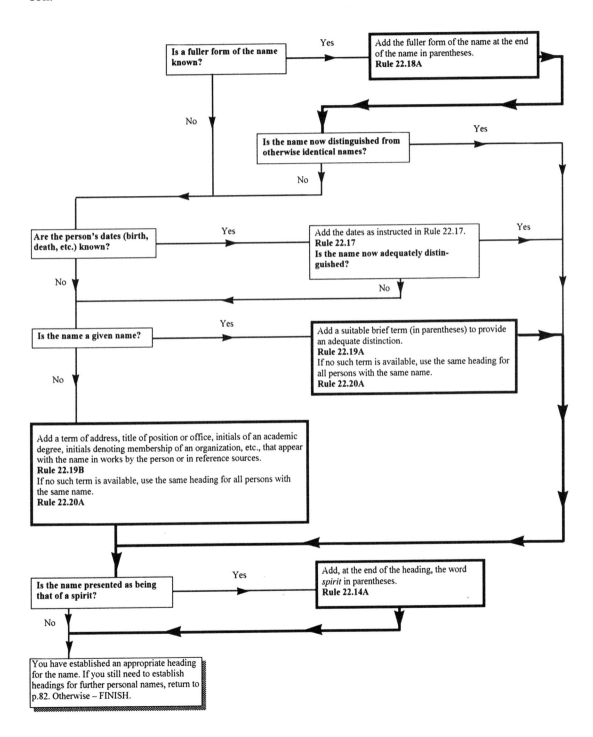